Visual and Performing Arts Framework

for California Public Schools ◆ Kindergarten Through Grade Twelve

Adopted by the
**California State Board of Education
on October 13, 1995**

Prepared under the direction of the
California State Board of Education

Developed by the
**Curriculum Development and Supplemental
Materials Commission**

Support provided by the
California Department of Education

Publishing Information

When the *Visual and Performing Arts Framework for California Public Schools* was adopted by the California State Board of Education on October 13, 1995, the members of the State Board were the following: Marion McDowell, President; Gerti B. Thomas, Vice-President; Kathryn Dronenburg, Jerry Hume, Yvonne W. Larsen, Dorothy J. Lee, Elaine Lokshin, S. William Malkasian, and Sanford C. Sigoloff.

This publication was edited by Sheila Bruton, working in cooperation with Diane Brooks, Administrator, and Mary Sprague, Consultant, Curriculum Frameworks and Instructional Resources Office; and Terry Givens, Consultant, Elementary Curriculum Development and Academic Expectations Unit. It was designed and prepared for photo-offset production by the staff of the Bureau of Publications, with the cover and interior design created and prepared by Juan Sanchez and Paul Lee. Typesetting was done by Carey Johnson. It was published by the Department of Education, 721 Capitol Mall, Sacramento, California (mailing address: P.O. Box 944272, Sacramento, CA 94244-2720), and was printed by the Office of State Printing and distributed under the provisions of the Library Distribution Act and *Government Code* Section 11096.

ISBN 0-8011-1261-3

Ordering Information

Copies of this publication are available for $14 each, plus sales tax for California residents, from the Bureau of Publications, Sales Unit, California Department of Education, P.O. Box 271, Sacramento, CA 95812-0271; FAX (916) 323-0823.

A partial list of other educational resources available from the Department appears on the inside of the back cover, where complete information on ordering is also provided. In addition, the *Educational Resources Catalog,* describing publications, videos, and other instructional media available from the Department, can be obtained without charge by writing to the address given above or by calling the Sales Unit at (916) 445-1260.

Photo Credits

We gratefully acknowlege the use in this publication of the photographs provided by the following: Donna Banning, p. vi; Bill Doggett, The Music Center Education Division, Los Angeles, pp. viii, 62; Helen K. Garber © 1995, (photographs are of students from the 1995 California State Summer School for the Arts), pp. 5, 9, 12, 23, 33, 35, 38, 41, 52, 56, 57, 59, 61, 70, 81, 91, 95; Jane Grossenbacher, Young Imaginations, p. 37; Lee Hanson, pp. 7, 16, 26, 29, 53, 77, 86, 90, 94, 97; Craig Schwartz, The Music Center Education Division, Los Angeles, pp. 2, 73, 79, 80; Beverly Tharp, pp. 71, 76; Liz Vargas, Young Imaginations, p. 18; and Kathi Kent Volzke, Courtesy of Orange County Performing Arts Center, pp. 32, 42, 75.

Notice

The guidance offered in the *Visual and Performing Arts Framework for California Public Schools* is not binding on local educational agencies or other entities. Except for the statutes, regulations, and court decisions that are referenced herein, the framework is exemplary, and compliance with it is not mandatory. (See *Education Code* Section 33308.5.)

Contents

Foreword v

Preface vii

Acknowledgments xi

Chapter 1. The Essential Ideas in Arts Education 1

Chapter 2. A Comprehensive Arts Program for All Students 15

Planning of a Comprehensive Arts Education Program 17

Delivery of a Comprehensive Arts Education Program 18

Four Components in a Comprehensive Arts Program 20

Three Levels of Schooling in a Comprehensive Arts Program 22

Arts for All Students in a Comprehensive Arts Program 24

Assessment in a Comprehensive Arts Program 24

Community Resources for Arts Education 26

Technology in the Service of the Arts 28

Chapter 3. Dance 31

The Four Components of Dance Education 34

Curriculum and Instruction in Dance Education 35

Students with Special Needs 37

Student Performances 37

Assessment in Dance Education 38

The Role of Technology in Dance Education 39

Teacher Preparation and Professional Development 39

Resources, Environment, Materials, and Equipment 40

Goals for Dance Education 42

Glossary: The Language of Dance 48

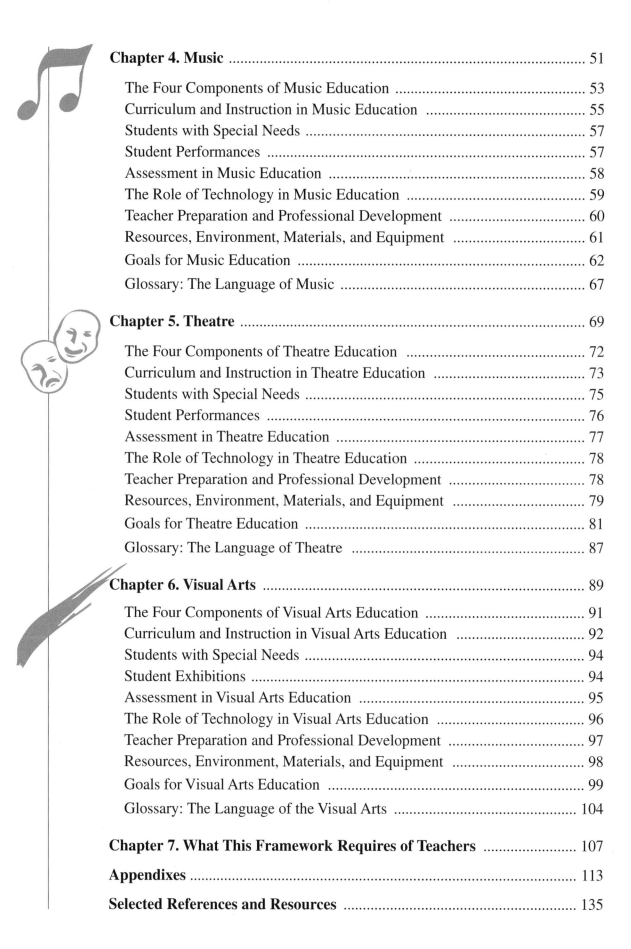

Chapter 4. Music 51

The Four Components of Music Education 53

Curriculum and Instruction in Music Education 55

Students with Special Needs 57

Student Performances 57

Assessment in Music Education 58

The Role of Technology in Music Education 59

Teacher Preparation and Professional Development 60

Resources, Environment, Materials, and Equipment 61

Goals for Music Education 62

Glossary: The Language of Music 67

Chapter 5. Theatre 69

The Four Components of Theatre Education 72

Curriculum and Instruction in Theatre Education 73

Students with Special Needs 75

Student Performances 76

Assessment in Theatre Education 77

The Role of Technology in Theatre Education 78

Teacher Preparation and Professional Development 78

Resources, Environment, Materials, and Equipment 79

Goals for Theatre Education 81

Glossary: The Language of Theatre 87

Chapter 6. Visual Arts 89

The Four Components of Visual Arts Education 91

Curriculum and Instruction in Visual Arts Education 92

Students with Special Needs 94

Student Exhibitions 94

Assessment in Visual Arts Education 95

The Role of Technology in Visual Arts Education 96

Teacher Preparation and Professional Development 97

Resources, Environment, Materials, and Equipment 98

Goals for Visual Arts Education 99

Glossary: The Language of the Visual Arts 104

Chapter 7. What This Framework Requires of Teachers 107

Appendixes 113

Selected References and Resources 135

Foreword

Two centuries ago John Adams wrote the following:

I must study politics and war that my [children] may have liberty to study mathematics and philosophy. My [children] ought to study mathematics and philosophy, geography, natural history, naval architecture, navigation, commerce, and agriculture in order to give their children a right to study painting, poetry, music, architecture, statuary, tapestry, and porcelain.

The California Department of Education and the California State Board of Education continue to support arts education for all students as a vital and fundamental part of the core curriculum. The arts foster students' abilities to develop problem-solving skills, flexibility, creativity, cooperative approaches, persistence, and responsibility as well as oral and written language skills. The arts provide a balance in the curriculum that is particularly important for the development of tomorrow's leaders. As Ernest Boyer, president of the Carnegie Foundation for the Advancement of Teaching, explains:

. . . The arts are one of mankind's most visual and essential forms of language, and if we do not educate our children in the symbol system called the arts, we will lose not only our culture and civility but our humanity as well.

In California we have led the way toward curriculum reform in arts education with the *Visual and Performing Arts Framework for California Public Schools, Kindergarten Through Grade Twelve,* published in 1982 and updated in 1989. This 1996 revision of the framework builds on the philosophy stated in previous frameworks and reinforces the 1989 California State Board of Education policy on arts education, which declares the arts to be "an integral part of basic education for all students in kindergarten through grade twelve."

At the national level the past few years have been momentous for arts education. The arts are included in the national goals for education; a consensus on the importance of arts education is embodied in the *National Standards for Arts Education;* an assessment in the arts by the National Assessment of Education Progress is expected in 1997; and conferences across the country have focused on the value of the arts both for the sake of the arts themselves and for their capacity to develop in students the skills, abilities, and personal qualities necessary for the twenty-first century. This renewed national focus, together with a new understanding of how children learn and the advances that have been made in technology and methods for assessing student progress, complements California's policy for arts education.

This framework outlines what students should know in the arts. It is organized around the vision of providing opportunities for all students to become responsible, creative, reasoning, understanding, and thoughtful citizens. The arts can be the motivating force that helps students reach their goals. One such student, Jose Oswaldo Villedas, an art student from an inner city high school, writes that "life without the arts would be intolerable."

Let us continue to work together to offer comprehensive arts education to all of California's youths, creating artistically rich schools and successful students.

DELAINE EASTIN

State Superintendent of Public Instruction

MARION McDOWELL

President, State Board of Education

Preface

*I*N California we consider the arts to be essential to the education of all students. Accordingly, this revised edition of the *Visual and Performing Arts Framework* clearly defines a balanced, comprehensive arts program for all those enrolled in kindergarten through grade twelve.

In February, 1994, the State Board of Education appointed a team of experts in the visual and performing arts to draft a revised framework. This framework committee was directed to maintain the general concepts and principles from the previous framework: specifically, the four disciplines of dance, music, theatre, and the visual arts as well as the four arts as discrete disciplines with commonalities of the four components of artistic perception, creative expression, historical and cultural context, and aesthetic valuing. In addition, they were asked to update five major areas in accordance with current research and practice: assessment in the arts, multicultural perspective, cognitive theory, curriculum integration, and technology in arts education.

Chapter 1 explains the value of arts education and lists the ten essential ideas of arts education. A powerful advocacy statement for arts education included in the chapter is an important addition to the document. Over the past several years, support for the arts as part of the core curriculum has increased based on growing research. National educational groups, such as the Council of Chief State School Officers, the National Parent Teacher Association, the National School Boards Association, and the American Council for the Arts, as well as American business leaders, support the value of the arts in education. For example, Jane L. Polin, Manager of the General Electric Foundation, has stated:

. . . We see a tremendous need for workers who are creative, analytical, disciplined, and self-confident. And we believe that hands-on participation in the arts is one of the best ways to develop these leadership abilities in young people.

Chapter 2 includes expanded definitions of the four arts components and guidelines for planning, delivering, and assessing a comprehensive arts program for all students. As in past frameworks there are separate chapters for each of the arts disciplines: dance, music, theatre, and visual arts. Each discipline chapter (chapters 3–6) includes content goals organized by grade-level spans (K–4, 5–8, 9–12 proficient, and 9–12 advanced) and by the four arts components to ensure a balance to the arts curriculum. Chapter 7, titled "What This Framework Requires of Teachers," was added to the framework to help school personnel frame the professional development needs for teachers of the arts.

In an effort to reinforce connections between the arts and other core subjects, examples of integrated instruction are highlighted as sidebars in each of the discipline chapters. Of special note is the sidebar in the visual arts chapter that directs the reader to a center section of visual works of art that explains connections with this framework and the *History–Social Science Framework.*

The center section of this framework provides illustrative examples of the variety of works of art that might be used in both a core and an integrated approach to teaching visual arts. One reason for including pieces in this section was an evident link between the

works of art and the grade-level course descriptions in the *History–Social Science Framework.* The study of such works of art not only exemplifies the work of a specific artist, an art style, or a technique but also provides insights into the time period, culture, or other topics being studied. Although the connection to history–social science is the most common one, some connections to literature, science, and other subjects are also noted. District curriculum specialists and classroom teachers are encouraged to develop similar examples for each of the arts disciplines and core subjects, kindergarten through grade twelve, using varied cultures, eras, and art forms.

As a result of districtwide assessment of how the current curriculum matches the goals established in the framework, the adoption of a formal school board policy and a multiple-year plan for the arts is recommended at the local level. The plan would include establishing curriculum goals; building support; identifying, allocating, and using resources; implementing programs for students; and providing staff development for administrators and teachers. Through assessment, thought is given to effective programs designed to enhance the abilities of all students, including those with special needs, the college bound, and the gifted and artistically talented.

This framework presents criteria for evaluating instructional resources, both print and nonprint, submitted for adoption in the four arts disciplines. It calls for resources that include all four arts components (artistic perception, creative expression, historical and cultural context, and aesthetic valuing) and provides opportunities to make connections among the four arts disciplines and to integrate the arts with the other core subjects.

Further, the framework recommends the implementation, at the school and district levels, of professional development programs that are supported by the administration and thereby ensure that those responsible for delivering the arts curriculum understand the unique qualities and content of the arts. Personnel resources for this effort include well-informed principals who promote arts education, credentialed arts instructors, trained classroom arts teachers, and local artists.

The framework recognizes the vital role that the arts play in the economic development of California, where the entertainment industry is well established. Spending on nonprofit arts organizations supports thousands of jobs and provides about $1 billion in income for the California economy each year. In Appendix C, the chart titled "Examples of Careers in the Visual and Performing Arts" contains numerous career titles and places where artists or those committed to the value of the arts might be employed.

State Superintendent of Public Instruction Delaine Eastin feels strongly about the power of the arts. For any school in the Challenge District Program, established in 1995, she is requiring a course in the visual and performing arts for all students as a condition of high school graduation.

Through a creative and inclusive visual and performing arts program that is well planned and is built on prior skills and knowledge, we hope that today's students will learn to participate in society in an intelligent way. Our wish is that they look at things carefully, hear things thoughtfully, feel things sensitively, and understand the role of the arts in the life of the individual and in the collective life of American culture.

RUTH McKENNA
Chief Deputy Superintendent
Instructional Services

PATRICIA H. NEWSOME
Deputy Superintendent,
Curriculum and Instructional
Leadership Branch

GLEN THOMAS
Executive Secretary
Curriculum Development and
Supplemental Materials Commission

DIANE L. BROOKS
Administrator
Curriculum Frameworks and
Instructional Resources Office

Acknowledgments

PREPARED under the direction of the California State Board of Education, this publication was developed by the Curriculum Development and Supplemental Materials Commission (Curriculum Commission). Of particular note was the guidance provided by:

Charlene Gould, Chair, Visual and Performing Arts Subject Matter Committee, Curriculum Development and Supplemental Materials Commission (1995); Ocean View School District

Katalin Stazer, Vice Chair, Visual and Performing Arts Subject Matter Committee, Curriculum Development and Supplemental Materials Commission (1995); Los Angeles Unified School District

The Curriculum Commission benefited from the work of the Visual and Performing Arts Framework and Criteria Committee, which consisted of 14 dedicated California arts educators and administrators. These individuals were responsible for developing the initial framework for presentation to the Curriculum Commission. This committee was chaired by:

Cris Guenter, California State University, Chico

The other committee members were:

Donna Banning, Orange Unified School District

Gabriel Bernstein, The California Arts Project

Beverley Bullis, Walnut Valley Unified School District

M. Kent Gregory, Garden Grove Unified School District

Lynn Hickey, Los Angeles Unified School District

Lois Hunter, Los Angeles High School for the Arts

David Kilpatrick, Los Angeles Unified School District

Mitsu Kumagai, The Redwood Arts Project

Yvonne McClung, San Francisco Unified School District

Lisa Roseman, Tustin Unified School District

Theresa Shellcroft, Hesperia Unified School District

James Thomas, Long Beach Unified School District

Susan Watts, Benicia Unified School District

Ruth Mitchell served as the writer for the Framework Committee.

California Department of Education staff members who contributed to developing the framework were:

Diane L. Brooks, Administrator, Curriculum Frameworks and Instructional Resources Office

Terry Givens, Consultant, Elementary Curriculum Development and Academic Expectations Office

Mary Sprague, Consultant, Curriculum Frameworks and Instructional Resources Office

Nancy Sullivan, Consultant, Curriculum Frameworks and Instructional Resources Office

Debbie Sweat, Analyst, Elementary Networks Office

Patty Taylor, Consultant, Middle Grades Curriculum Development and Academic Expectations Office

Glen Thomas, Assistant Superintendent and Director, Elementary Teaching and Learning Division

Support staff members were:

Valarie Bliss, Curriculum Frameworks and Instructional Resources Office

Billie Hackett, Legal Office

The chair of the Curriculum Commission at the time this framework was approved was:

Eugene Flores (Chair, 1995), University of California, Los Angeles.

Other members of the Visual and Performing Arts Subject Matter Committee of the Curriculum Commission responsible for overseeing the development of the framework were:

Jerry Treadway (Vice Chair, 1995), San Diego State University

Kirk Ankeney, San Diego Unified School District

Michele Garside, Butte County Office of Education

Elaine Rosenfield, San Luis Coastal Unified School District

The remaining members of the Curriculum Commission were:

Del Alberti, Lodi Unified School District

Lillian Vega Castaneda, California State University, San Marcos

Gus T. Dalis, Los Angeles County Office of Education

Bruce Fisher, Fortuna Union Elementary School District

Mary Jew, San Francisco Unified School District

Gerard A. Klimbal, Merced Union High School District

Charles J. Kloes, Beverly Hills Unified School District

Janny Latno-Yamate, Vallejo City Unified School District

Sharon Valear Williams Robinson, Los Angeles Unified School District

Glen Thomas, Executive Secretary, Curriculum Commission

Special thanks are extended to:

Eliott Eisner, Professor of Education and Art, School of Education, Stanford University, for his insightful vision paper titled "A Vision for the Arts in California Schools: Doing Right by Our Children," which is included in Appendix A; and for comments and direction on how to express clearly the important concepts in this framework.

Arts experts who donated their time to provide an extensive review of each of the four discipline chapters and the resource list were:

Cris Guenter, California State University, Chico

Lois Harrison, University of the Pacific

Charlotte Kay Motter, Chair, Legislative Action Coalition for Arts Education

Judy Scalin, Loyola Marymount University

Rose Messina, Teacher, Sunkist Elementary School, Hueneme Elementary School District, and **Karen Hafenstein,** Site Director of the Northeast California Arts Project (TCAP), assisted with the technology sections of the framework. **Terry Givens,** Consultant, Elementary Curriculum Development and Academic Expectations Office, provided extensive writing support on the final versions of the framework.

Chapter 1

The Essential Ideas in Arts Education

A teacher affects eternity; he can never tell where his influence stops.

—Henry Adams, *The Education of Henry Adams*

EDUCATION in the arts is essential for all students. California's public school system must provide a balanced curriculum, with the arts as a part of the core for all students, kindergarten through grade twelve, no matter what the students' abilities, language capacities, or special needs happen to be.

Each of the arts disciplines (dance, music, theatre, and the visual arts) maintains a rich body of knowledge that enables students to understand their world in ways that support and enhance their learning in other core subjects. In addition, through this rich body of knowledge, students learn how each of the arts contributes to their own sensitivity of the aesthetic qualities of life. Students learn to see what they look at, hear what they listen to, feel what they touch, and understand more clearly what they integrate into their own experience. Through viewing such images as the flag paintings of Childe Hassam, students can understand the exuberance of being in or witnessing a parade. By hearing Taiko drumming, students feel the power of rhythm, pattern, and percussion. Through engaging in movement in ways taught by Alvin Ailey, students come to understand the potential of their own bodies. And by reading and reflecting on plays by Wendy Wasserstein, students create new meanings based on their experience and past knowledge.

In an address to the President's Committee on the Arts and Humanities in 1991, Harold M. Williams, President and Chief Executive Officer of the J. Paul Getty Trust, described the vital role of the arts: "The arts are a basic and central medium of human communication and understanding. The arts are how we talk to each other. They are the language of civilizations—past and present—through which we express our anxieties, our hungers, our hopes, and our discoveries."[1]

Gaining insights into past cultures through each of the arts is only a part of the story. Students need to be able to discern their own lives and cultures more clearly and to make sense out of the sometimes overwhelming barrage of images and sounds that come through the media. The arts help people learn how to talk to one another across the multiplicity of languages that are spoken.

Study of the arts helps all students exercise their cognitive reasoning and their intuition. As Williams stated, "Art instruction that involves students in analyzing works of art, whether their own or others, requires functioning at the highest cognitive levels of mental activity."[2] For example, to create or perform a work of art successfully in dance, music, theatre, or the visual arts, students must think about what they are doing, how they are doing it, and what they find to be the meaning inherent in the work. Students' cognitive skills, such as language fluency and reading comprehension, are enhanced as they talk and write about the works of art they have created and performed. Other cognitive concepts, such as symbolic representation, occur when one object is used to represent another or, for example, when student dancers represent objects or events in nature through movement. When students talk about works of art and performances, they engage in the process of analysis. When they discuss relationships between works of art, they synthesize perceptions and information about those works and their own experiences.

This framework is based on three convictions. The first is that the arts have an *intrinsic* value, which makes them indispensable in the center of every student's education. Second, the arts have an *instrumental* value; that is, they assist students in learning other subjects and disciplines. Third, the arts have an *enduring* value; in an educated society everyone has the knowledge and background that allows them to experience and enjoy the arts throughout their lives. Because of the contribution of each of these values to the cognitive, emotional, and spiritual development of each child, the arts must be a part of the basic educational program for all students.

The most important contribution of the arts to education is their ability to improve the way we teach and learn. . . . Here's why:

- The arts inspire self-confidence and help keep kids interested in school.
- The arts help energize the school environment.
- The arts help kids develop critical skills for life and work.
- The arts improve student performance in other subject areas.
- The arts expose kids to a range of cultures and points of view.
- The arts can reach hard-to-reach students.

And let's not forget that the arts are something a child should learn to understand and appreciate in and of themselves—not necessarily as a means to an end but for the sheer enjoyment of a great play, a dance, a painting, or a song.

Adapted from *Performing Wonders, Kids and the Arts: A Broadcaster Guide to Teaching Children About the Arts.* Washington, D.C.: The Kennedy Center and National Association of Broadcasters, n.d.

---

[1] Harold M. Williams, "The Language of Civilization: the Vital Role of the Arts in Education." Address given before the President's Committee on the Arts and the Humanities, New York City, 1991.

[2] Williams, 3.

In a paper titled "A Vision for the Arts in California Schools: Doing Right by Our Children," written expressly for this framework and reprinted in Appendix A, Elliot Eisner discusses the meaning and implications of several major ideas crucial to an understanding of the essential nature of the arts in education:

> One of these is that policy decisions concerning what shall be taught in California schools are, at base, decisions about the kinds of opportunities children will have to invent their own minds. Second, the justification for the inclusion of any subject in the school curriculum ultimately rests upon a conception of how minds are developed and how meanings are made. Education is about the creation of mind and the expansion of meaning. Third, human experience depends initially upon the extent to which we have refined our sensory system. It is through the refined senses that we get in touch with the world. This, in turn, makes it possible to form concepts. Fourth, once concepts are formed, they can be recalled or treated imaginatively. The imaginative treatment of our conceptual life makes it possible to create new possibilities that can be pursued. Fifth, the public realization of these possibilities requires the ability to skillfully use the various symbol systems or forms of representation that the culture itself makes available. Students, in a sense, become multiliterate as they learn how to use a variety of symbolic forms as means for either recovering or creating new meanings.

The ideas embodied in this framework are that the arts have inherent and shared aspects which characterize their power to reach the perceptual, intellectual, cultural, and spiritual dimensions of human experience, as discussed by Eisner. They project a vision for the arts in California schools, kindergarten through grade twelve—a vision which places the arts' profound insights into the human condition at the heart of education. Arts education for all students in California is built around ten essential ideas.

All of the arts depend upon the use of the human's most exquisite capacity —judgment. . . . They are fundamental resources through which the world is viewed, meaning is created, and the mind is developed.

—Elliot Eisner

Essential Ideas in Arts Education

1. The arts are core subjects.

2. Arts instruction encompasses four components.

3. The arts enrich and are enriched by the other subjects.

4. The arts promote creativity, thinking, and joy.

5. The arts offer different ways to make meaning.

6. The arts reflect and influence cultures.

7. The arts promote aesthetic literacy.

8. Assessment is inherent in the arts.

9. Technology expands the arts.

10. The arts prepare students for full participation in society.

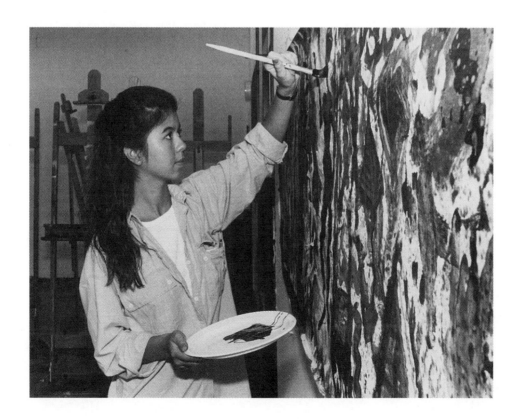

1. The Arts Are Core Subjects

The arts are core subjects because each of the arts contains a distinct body of knowledge and skills that enables students to understand their world. Substantive instruction is required in the theory and practice of the individual disciplines of dance, music, theatre, and the visual arts. Knowledge about theory in an arts discipline is often manifest in the skills involved in the practice of the art form.

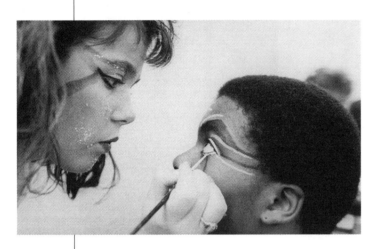

Study of the arts refines a student's ability to perceive aesthetically; to make connections between works of art and the lives people live; to discuss visual, kinesthetic, and auditory relationships; to locate artworks in time and place; to make judgments about artworks and give reasons for those judgments; and to continue to search the sensory world for meaning. It cultivates an ability to imagine a world that is not now and develops a student's willingness to explore ambiguousness, multiple conceptions of the world, and multiple solutions to issues.

For example, a study of the Bayeux Tapestry, which depicts events leading to the Norman invasion of England and the victory of Hastings in A.D. 1066, tells students about specific historical events. It also informs students about scientific phenomena (the appearance of Halley's comet in the same year) and the status of women artists in the Middle Ages (the 75 embroidered scenes were surely executed by a group of women artists). Through reading and writing about this work of art, students not only understand visual arts principles, such as pattern, use of color, and narration, but also gain a deeper understanding of the way in which people lived in the early Middle Ages in France and how different the world is now than it was then. Through careful study of artworks, such as tapestries and quilts, one can hear civilizations speak through the ages and understand the connections of past lives to present and future ones.

Academic rigor is a basic characteristic of education in the arts and includes active learning through the practice, rehearsal, and creation or performance of works of art; reading about the arts and artists in fiction and nonfiction; writing about the arts in research papers, using primary sources, and in thoughtful essays or journal reflections on one's observations, feelings, and ideas about the arts; and participating in arts criticism based on knowledge, criteria, and multiple responses.

2. Arts Instruction Encompasses Four Components

The content of this framework encompasses the disciplines of dance, music, theatre, and the visual arts. These arts disciplines have in common the following four components, which bring instructional balance to an arts curriculum and conform with the philosophy established in the 1982 and 1989 frameworks for visual and performing arts:

- *Artistic perception*—processing sensory information through elements unique to the arts
- *Creative expression*—producing works in the arts, either by creating them or by performing original or existing works
- *Historical and cultural context*—understanding and appreciating the arts in the time and place of their creation

- *Aesthetic valuing*—analyzing, making informed judgments, and pursuing meaning in the arts

A complete and comprehensive arts education includes each component in the instruction of the arts discipline. Each component contains a body of knowledge and skills unique to the arts discipline and common among all four arts. A fundamental goal embodied in this framework is that every student in every California school must experience each arts discipline and the breadth of all four components in each discipline during each year of school. (See Chapter 2, "A Comprehensive Arts Program for All Students," for an expanded discussion of the four components.)

3. The Arts Enrich and Are Enriched by Other Subjects

The arts enrich and are enriched by other subjects because of the deeper insights gained through understanding the connections between and among the arts and other subjects.

The arts enrich other subjects, such as history, health education, geography, science, or literature, by providing students with insights into a period of time from a variety of points of view and an understanding of the way in which the arts both reflect and influence a society's beliefs. Connections of the arts to other subjects provide students with information with which to make judgments that validate or challenge their perceptions. Connections and judgments together allow students to acquire meaningful knowledge about themselves; other people in different times and places; and issues, events, and experiences. For example, when studying the Great Depression in the United States, students who have also studied the Federal Theatre Project of the Works Progress Administration and the influence of the "Living Newspaper" series will have a

deeper understanding of a particular time in the history of this country. The "Living Newspaper" series of productions focused on the viewpoints of workers rather than on those of the managers.

The arts are enriched by other subjects because they provide students with a way of seeing another body of knowledge from the viewpoint of an artist, musician, composer, actor, playwright, dancer, or choreographer. For example, the Vietnam War Memorial, designed by Maya Lin, is a piece of architectural sculpture that connects an event in American history with a specific site and design. Why does this work of art speak to its viewers so powerfully? Parts of the answer are embedded in the artist's selection of a site between the Lincoln monument and the United States Capitol, the sculpture's below-the-ground location, the specific design of the sculpture and the artist's use of materials, the sculpture's reference to a particular war, and the issues connecting the Vietnam War to the national consciousness. Study of this piece of art, including its triangular shapes, its mirror-like black surface, the designer's use of space, and knowledge of the healing power of the arts through the use of individual names, cannot be effectively accomplished without reference to a study of history, mathematics, and literature.

4. The Arts Promote Creativity, Thinking, and Joy

Creativity involves knowing enough about the ideas of the art form and the precision and execution of artistic technique to manipulate the elements and principles of the arts discipline. David Perkins writes of looking for "the art in art,"[3] by which he means learning how to perceive the meaning found in technical choices, such as juxtapositions, contrasts, changes, similarities. While students respond emotionally to a work of art, they can also think about how it produced the effect on their feelings. In other words, what lines, colors, sounds, movements were placed together or repeated or changed to give the work meaning?

When words are no longer adequate, when our passion is greater than we are able to express in a usual manner, people turn to art. Some people go to the canvas and paint; some stand up and dance. But we all go beyond our normal means of communicating and this is the common human experience for all people on this planet.

—Murray Sidlin, conductor

Knowledge and *thinking* are required to understand the art of art. Participating in and learning about dance, music, theatre, and visual arts unite the mind and the body. Each of the arts has intellectual and emotional components; therefore, the whole self is not

_____
[3] "Art as Understanding," in *The Arts and Cognition.* Edited by David Perkins and Barbara Leondar. Baltimore: Johns Hopkins University Press, 1977, p. 119.

only involved but also expanded, even constructed, by experiences in the arts.

The arts develop the students' abilities to think, observe, create, organize thoughts and feelings, assess critically, and respond in predictable and unpredictable ways. The arts provide opportunities for students to use their imaginations.

The arts bring a heightened sense of *joy,* well-being, and exhilaration to people's daily lives: surprise when something unexpected happens, such as the clear, clean sound of Wynton Marsalis' trumpet as it soars over a Bach concerto or growls over a 12-bar phrase of Louis Armstrong; recognition of the pointed humor in a Gilbert and Sullivan opera; and realization that an August Wilson play connects to one's own life.

People find joy also in the meaning the arts give to their lives and in the knowledge that, through the arts, they become a part of a human tradition in a search for meaning—a search that stretches from petroglyphs and cave drawings, rhythms on animal bones, ritual dances, and masked ceremonies through neon sculpture, electronic keyboards, hip-hop, and the theatre of the absurd to future, yet-unknown forms of expression.

5. The Arts Offer Different Ways to Make Meaning

The arts encourage and reward meaning, which cannot always be expressed in words or numbers, and thus keep some students in school simply by allowing them to express themselves in different ways. The arts can also provide an alternative access to words or numbers that may help some students to succeed.

Interest is frequently a matter of personal inclination. However, interest may reflect a different kind of intelligence. Howard Gardner, codirector of Project Zero at Harvard University, suggests that human intelligence has more forms than the linguistic and logical-mathematical intelligences that are usually rewarded in school.[4] In addition to those two intelligences, Gardner proposes musical, spatial, bodily-kinesthetic, and inter- and intrapersonal intelligences. (Please refer to chapters 3 through 6 for descriptions of the ways in which the theory of multiple intelligences is embodied in each arts discipline.)

The student's mind does not wait for facts in measured amounts but rather seeks information actively. The human mind constructs meaning from the moment of birth and continues to do so throughout life. Learning is a process of assimilating new information and skills so that meanings already in the mind are challenged. In this model the mind engages in interaction with new material for learning to occur.

The arts are excellent examples of multiple, active ways in which to make meaning. The expression of meaning in early pictures, dances, role-playing, and musical pieces leads naturally to the search for a technique to express more complex meaning. The arts cannot be acquired passively; there must be active participation. A student comes into the arts with meanings already attached to the words *dance, music, theatre*, and *visual art*. These ideas are modified by the trial-and-error experience of creating or performing; perceiving as a dancer, musician, actor, or painter; connecting meaning with other ideas, issues, and events in another time and place; and engaging in the constant reevaluation that is the essence of artistic production.

6. The Arts Reflect and Influence Cultures

California schools already serve students from more cultures throughout the world

---

[4] The original exposition of the theory of multiple intelligences is found in Howard Gardner, *Frames of Mind: The Theory of Multiple Intelligences.* New York: Basic Books, 1983, 1985, and 1993. There are now many popular expositions of the theory.

than those from which the nation's founders came. The voices of Californians whose families and cultures bring the world to this state and to the American culture are not merely additions to the chorus; they enhance its nature. When peoples, cultures, and societies join together, they speak with an expanded voice and enrich each other through the unique lens that the arts, in all their significance, depth, and shapes of meaning, provide. The arts have the power to bring all Americans to the same high plane of human understanding.

Because of these facts and assumptions and the richness that many cultures bring to California, this framework does not include an isolated section on multiculturalism; nor does it treat any group's contributions in isolation. Respect for the multiplicity of cultures pervades the entire framework. In this broad view of culture, the curriculum is transformed so that students experience the arts and their four components from the perspectives of the American culture and of worldwide ethnic, racial, religious, and cultural groups.

The arts reflect the times and cultures of the people who created them. The arts also influenced, and continue to influence, the societies and cultures in which they were created. They serve as a living record of their time—a means of bringing people into more vivid contact with past civilizations and present societies. As students explore the arts, they begin to understand how cultures, past and present, communicate through dance, music, theatre, and visual forms.

In a multicultural approach students research and acquire information about people through their arts: the creators of the art-works or performances, the functions they served, the contexts in which they were made, and the messages (if any) they convey to society. The arts provide insights into the past and present and reflect continuity and change.

The arts open avenues for acquiring knowledge of the history, experiences, and contributions of cultures throughout the world and for learning about the cultural heritage of the United States. Through the arts students learn about people and cultures because society enshrines what it believes and values in its arts.

The arts of religious and ethnic groups are explored as an important aspect of the regular curriculum throughout the year. The study of the influence of religion on art, sculpture, architecture, dance, theatre, and music reveals the beliefs and values of the time in which the works were created and the impact of religion on the lives of men and women and on societies. Although the political heritage of Americans prevents the teaching of religion as faith in public schools, students should still be taught about religious art. Because religious themes are prevalent in the arts throughout the world, an avoidance of teaching about the influence of religion would severely impoverish learning in the arts.

As the publication adopted by the State Board of Education titled *Moral, Civic, and Ethical Education and Teaching About Religion* . . . (1995) makes clear, teaching about religion is permissible and, according to various court interpretations, is so noted in the U.S. Constitution and the Constitution of the State of California. The *Education Code* and opinions issued by the Attorney General of California address the teaching about religion.

The important word to remember when teaching about religion in the classroom is the word *about*. (Refer to Appendix D for more guidance on this topic.) The following statements from the document titled *Religion in the Public School Curriculum: Questions and Answers* will help teachers distinguish between teaching *about* religion and religious *indoctrination:*

- The school's approach to religion is academic, not devotional.
- The school may strive for student awareness of religions but should not press for student acceptance of any one religion.
- The school may sponsor study about religion but may not sponsor the practice of religion.
- The school may expose students to a diversity of religious views but may not impose any particular view.
- The school may educate about all religions but may not promote or denigrate any religion.
- The school may inform the student about various beliefs but should not seek to conform him or her to any particular belief.

Note: Copies of *Religion in the Public School Curriculum: Questions and Answers* may be obtained from the California 3Rs Project: Rights, Responsibilities, and Respect (sponsored by the Curriculum and Instruction Steering Committee), 777 Camino Pescadero, Isla Vista, CA 93117.

7. The Arts Promote Aesthetic Literacy

Works of art communicate in images, metaphors, sounds, and movements. An aesthetically literate person explores and understands the fullness of many forms of communication, including reading, writing, and the specialized language of the arts.

As noted in the publication titled *Toward Civilization: A Report on Arts Education,* students learn the essence of modern civilization through a basic arts education; they also learn about the civilizations that have contributed to theirs and about the more distant civilizations that have enriched the world as a whole.[5] Knowledge of the earliest civilizations is acquired through artistic activities, such as the paintings of the caves of Lascaux, the ancient bronzes and pottery figures of pre-Shang China, and the pyramids of Egypt. A significant portion of the heritage of Greek civilization is disclosed through the epics of Homer and the Parthenon. The bronze sculptures of Benin tell almost all that is known of the great African empire that antedated Spain's by nearly 100 years. And many of the achievements of the Maya would be lost without the discovery of the great temples overgrown by jungles in Mexico and Central America. The knowledge and understanding of such supreme achievements form the foundation of aesthetic and historical literacy.

For students to become aesthetically literate, mere exposure to the best of the arts or to an abundance of information about past and present civilizations and their accomplishments is not enough. The reflection on, analysis of, and synthesis of that information and constant attempts to find meaning in the information and to put it into realistic, meaningful contexts constitute the attributes of an aesthetically literate person.

[5] *Toward Civilization: A Report on Arts Education.* Washington, D.C.: National Endowment for the Arts, 1988.

Marcia Eaton proposes the following definitions of aesthetic experience and aesthetic value: "Aesthetic experience is experience of intrinsic features of things or events traditionally recognized as worthy of attention and reflection. Aesthetic value is the value a thing or event has due to its capacity to evoke pleasure that is recognized as arising from features in the object traditionally considered worthy of attention and reflection."[6] That is, aesthetic value is a matter of both individual response to things or events and the social and cultural contexts of those responses.

The aesthetically literate person understands the way in which aesthetic value is derived from experience and how that value depends on one's particular cultural traditions.

The aesthetically literate person also knows that the artistic dimensions of existence have meaning for every sphere of human endeavor . . . and that a refined aesthetic sensibility can as easily lead to a cure for cancer as to the composition of a great symphony.

—James Fenwick

---

8. Assessment Is Inherent in the Arts

Students are assessed in the arts to learn more about what they know and can do, to use that information to improve curriculum and instruction, and to ensure accountability. Some of the types of performance assessments, such as portfolios, projects, exhibitions, and reflections, are also a part of the language of the arts.

Learning the arts consists largely of trying something out (playing, improvising a few steps, drawing a sketch, blocking out a move on the stage), then modifying it after reflecting on the goal and what is necessary to

[6] Marcia Eaton, *Basic Issues in Aesthetics.* Belmont, Calif.: Wadsworth Publishing Co., 1988, p. 143.

attain it. Self-assessment and collaborative assessment guide the artist or performer through this process. The student has an ideal in mind, a certain meaning or intent that must be conveyed in a certain style, and hones every detail to achieve the perfect communication. Assessment in the arts fosters reflection and the ability to think and write about what has been learned, to assimilate those learnings, and to base future action on artistic perception and aesthetic valuing.

Work has already begun at state and local levels on the design of multiple tools, including assessment portfolios, projects, and performances, to assess student learning in the arts. In the framework the assumption is made that the arts will be formally assessed in the future by a California statewide system of assessment. (See Chapter 2, "A Comprehensive Arts Program for All Students," for additional information on assessment in the arts.)

9. Technology Expands the Arts

Through the years technology has provided tools that enhance and expand all the arts disciplines. For example, drawing pencils, musical instruments, stage lights, and recorded media are all forms of technology.

Computer and multimedia technology broaden the possibilities in the arts. Many computer programs are available for composing music, developing animation, analyzing works of art, creating graphic designs, designing sets, writing choreography, computerizing stage lighting and scenery, and playing electronic instruments. Further, telecommunications allow the sharing of all of these developments with a larger audience. For example, students across the United States can collaborate on playwriting or choreographing a dance on-line. Two students can improvise jazz together, one on the East Coast and one on the West Coast. Visual art can be shared around the world and be revised or added to by students in diverse settings.

Electronic technologies extend the horizons of the arts in directions not yet imagined. The arts community welcomes the opportunities that technologies present. Before technology made electronic recording a possibility, all music was played for a live audience. The vast expansion in musical experience that recordings brought is being replicated by similar breakthroughs in new electronic technology. Student field trips to private and public art collections and museums are a valuable experience for students. Now telecommunications allows students to visit museums and art collections any place in the world through the World Wide Web (WWW) and the Internet.

Technology remains what it has always been—a tool. But it is a tool that can enlarge the scope of the arts beyond anything known at the moment. Although no one can accurately predict the future, technology will continue to play an important role in the arts and in arts education of the future. The use of technology throughout the grades is essential to enhance student learning of the arts, to enfranchise the imagination, and to expand human expression through the arts. (See Chapter 2 for additional information on technology in the arts.)

10. The Arts Prepare Students for Full Participation in Society

The arts play a vital role in the flourishing economic development of California. Arts education provides direct training for jobs in the arts industry. In 1994 the California Arts Council published *The Arts: A Competitive Advantage for California,* which presented an overview of the status of the arts industry and its economic impact on California. Some of the data demonstrate the way in which the arts enrich the quality of life in California and contribute to California's economic growth and the creation of jobs.[7] For example:

- Spending on the nonprofit arts directly and indirectly supports more than 115,000 full-time and part-time jobs in California and adds $1 billion in income to the California economy.

- A survey of people working in the arts in Los Angeles County shows that they earn an average of $38,000 a year and are involved in their communities (86 percent of those surveyed vote).

- The first automotive design studio of any automaker in the world employing more than 400 people was opened in the 1970s by Toyota Motor Corporation and was located in California to be near a nonprofit arts institution—Pasadena's Art Center College of Design.

- The design and manufacture of musical instruments, with accompanying electronics and accessories, is a $500 million industry in California.

Education in the arts is preparation for work in any field according to the literature on workplace training. An influential publication on the relationship of school to competence in the workplace is titled *What Work Requires of Schools,* first published in 1991 by the Secretary of Labor's Commission on Achieving Necessary Skills (SCANS).[8] Workplace know-how is defined by five competencies: ability to use resources; interpersonal skills; manipulation of information; understanding of systems; and use of appropriate technology. Arts education applications provide for all five of the identified competencies. One illustration is the *manipulation of information:* information about technique, content, ourselves, and others is always necessary to the arts. Another illustration is the *understanding of systems,* which underlies the comprehension of any complex artifact or performance. For example, a studio classroom, band, orchestra, or dance troupe is a system, and students soon understand how it works and their role in it.

Life without industry is guilt; industry without art is brutality.

—John Ruskin (1819–1900)

Participation in society is about more than entering into the workforce. It is also about enjoying the rich benefits of life in the United States, engaging in its multiple opportunities for self-expression, undertaking the responsibilities of a thoughtful member of a diverse society, and delighting in the creative efforts of others. Arts students are able to participate in society in an intelligent way by looking at things carefully, hearing things thoughtfully, and feeling things sensitively. When students have access to the arts throughout their school years, they have a greater opportunity to grow as creative, intellectual, and spiritual human beings.

---

[7] *The Arts: A Competitive Advantage for California.* Prepared by the Policy Economics Group. Sacramento: KMPG Peat Marwick and The California Arts Council, 1994.

[8] *What Work Requires of Schools: A SCANS Report for America 2000.* Upland, Pa.: Diane Publishing Co., 1993.

Chapter 2

A Comprehensive Arts Program for All Students

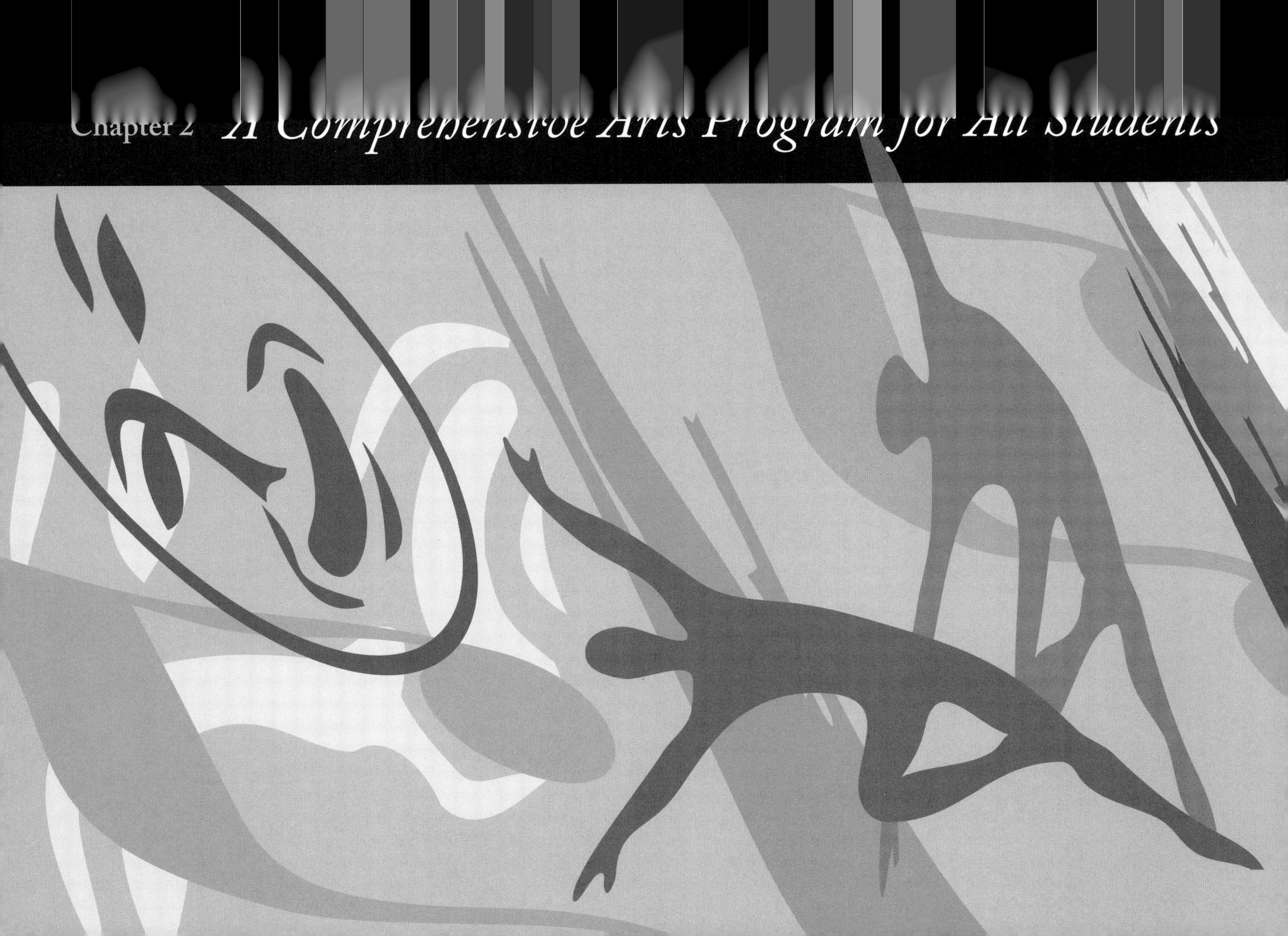

Art attempts to find in the universe, in matter as well as in the facts of life, what is fundamental, enduring, essential.

—Saul Bellow (1915–)

THE careful planning, delivery, and assessment of a comprehensive arts education program is important for the education of all students. Included in this chapter are descriptions of the following:

- Planning of a comprehensive arts education program

- Delivery of a comprehensive arts education program

- Four components in a comprehensive arts program (artistic perception, creative expression, historical and cultural context, and aesthetic valuing)

- Three levels of schooling (elementary, middle, secondary) in a comprehensive arts program

- Students with special needs in a comprehensive arts program

- Assessment as a part of a comprehensive arts program

- Community resources for arts education

- Technology in the service of the arts

Teachers, artists who teach in the schools, and those who plan or develop local arts education programs will all benefit from this chapter because it places all the arts in the context of comprehensive, basic education. In addition, administrators, superintendents, principals, curriculum developers, and school board members will find the descriptions in this chapter helpful as they plan arts education programs for all students.

Planning of a Comprehensive Arts Education Program

An integral part of the success of any educational program is the degree of county, district, and schoolwide collaboration, parent involvement, and college, university, and community participation in the process of program design and implementation. All students benefit when the school board and district administration, parents, school, and community together acknowledge that the arts are basic in education; that they value the arts; and that they consider each arts discipline along with the other core academic subjects in planning for facilities, resources, professional development, and assessment. The implementation of a comprehensive arts curriculum is the responsibility of many parties.

According to the State Board of Education's Arts Education Policy, adopted in July, 1989, "districts should develop a policy, allocate resources, and carry out a plan to provide a high-quality comprehensive arts education program for all students based on the adopted visual and performing arts curriculum resource documents." The publication titled *Handbook for Planning an Effective Visual and Performing Arts Program* describes effective models for planning and implementing high-quality comprehensive arts programs.[1] The school board and school district administration have responsibility for adopting an arts policy in support of arts education; developing a district plan for implementation; allocating instructional and personnel resources; and ensuring that there is a district curriculum for dance, music, theatre, and visual arts.

The site-level administrator is crucial to the planning and success of the visual and performing arts program at the school. It is not necessary for an administrator to be an expert in the arts, but it is important for that person to understand the value of arts education; to be an advocate for the arts with the school staff, parents, and the community; and to set in motion a planning process that includes broad-based representation.

The *Handbook* describes the following three-committee process for planning or improving a comprehensive arts education program at the school:

- The Organizing Committee is a small, dedicated group that identifies the vision for arts education, begins to determine needs, and builds an advocacy group.

- The Planning Committee, an expanded group that may include members of the Organizing Committee, completes an assessment of the current program; determines specific goals, needs, and priorities; and develops a long-range plan.

---

[1] *Handbook for Planning an Effective Visual and Performing Arts Program* (February, 1990), pp. 18–19. The document was commissioned by the Curriculum and Instruction Steering Committee of the California Association of County Superintendents of Schools. It is available from the Tulare County Office of Education, Education Building, County Civic Center, Visalia CA 93291-4581.

- The Implementing Committee, which may include members of the other committees as active or advisory members, involves those who are directly responsible for program implementation, such as teachers, district-level staff, administrators, artists, and arts providers.

In small schools or rural areas, an alternate model is for one committee to play various roles at different times in the process, with additional district staff, educators, and community members included for specific tasks.

In addition to establishing a planning and implementation process, the site administrator ensures that the arts are included in the basic education of all students by:

- Designating planning time

- Providing access to each arts discipline through the scheduling of both teachers and students in subject-centered classes

- Allowing opportunities for teachers to meet across grade levels and subject areas for planning

- Ensuring that the total curriculum provides opportunities for integration of the arts

- Advocating to parents and community members the importance of the arts for all students

- Providing opportunities for exhibitions and performances of works in progress and the final products as educational experiences embedded in complete programs

It is the responsibility of the education community at large to see that arts education is firmly embedded in the district curriculum and the instructional program of the school. The product is an artistically rich school, and the beneficiaries are artistically and aesthetically literate students.

Delivery of a Comprehensive Arts Education Program

A comprehensive arts education program for all students, kindergarten through grade twelve, is composed of three modes of instruction: (1) subject-centered arts instruction in dance, music, theatre, or visual arts; (2) instruction connecting the arts disciplines; and (3) instruction connecting the arts and other core subjects. Students need to understand the essential elements, knowledge, and skills of the arts discipline in focus. In addition, they experience the emotion and thought communicated by the arts and learn how the arts permeate all human activity and affect and are affected by historical events and social and cultural affairs.

Subject-centered arts instruction focuses on developing foundation skills in an arts discipline. For example, students can best be helped to learn the essentials of music and be taught to play an instrument when they study the instrument apart from other subjects. Through subject-centered instruction students develop knowledge in the breadth of all components of the discipline. Such instruction is essential at advanced levels, when students may have decided to specialize in one of the arts. In a comprehensive arts program, subject-centered instruction provides foundation skills and knowledge in each of the arts; ongoing development in the arts discipline preferred by the student; and a solid basis for a career in one of the arts, for lifelong enjoyment, and for continued learning.

Instruction connecting the arts disciplines ties each art with one or more of the other arts disciplines in a well-planned, meaningful, and focused way. Knowledge and skills of two or more arts disciplines are used in ways that are mutually reinforcing and demonstrate the underlying unity of the arts. The knowledge and skills of the respective arts disciplines may be so intertwined that learning in each discipline occurs simultaneously.

At the middle and high school levels, teachers of the arts should cooperate in the planning and delivery of mutually reinforcing programs. For example, high school music and dance teachers collaborate on the development of a sequence of lessons focusing on twentieth-century music and dance. Dance students learn the dance style of Martha Graham, and music students learn the musical structures of Arnold Schoenberg. Each group culminates its explorations by composing and choreographing its own works and then presenting them in a recital of both disciplines performed separately and together. The benefits to teaching and learning derived from this kind of collaboration are the involvement of students and teachers working together toward a common goal, the cooperation that takes place through the interaction of dancers and musicians, the opportunity to learn basic ideas about another art form, and the knowledge and skills acquired to create a successful performance.

Instruction connecting the arts and other core subjects ties the arts to other core subjects in substantive ways that strengthen the instructional goals in each subject. For example, an eleventh grade U.S. history class studies the Harlem Renaissance. By exploring the music of William Grant Still and Duke Ellington, the writings of James Weldon Johnson and Countee Cullen, and the visual art of Aaron Douglas and Augusta Savage, as well as the historical and social phenomena of Marcus Garvey and the Great Migration, students gain a greater depth of understanding about an important period in American history.

I urge you to hold fast to the value, strength, and clarity that the arts have brought to your lives, and fight to bring this power into the lives of the children in our nation's schools today. Do it in partnership, do it with compassion and do it with imagination. Fight to bring the arts, as subject, teacher, pleasure and inspiration more deeply into the lives of our children.

—Ramon C. Cortines
former Chancellor, New York City Public Schools

In another example a primary classroom teacher collaborates with specialist colleagues in mathematics and dance. Students practice, create, and perform dances in accordance with the mathematical concepts of addition and subtraction. They use their bodies to duplicate mathematics problems, then solve them kinesthetically as well as mentally.

Building connections through the arts gives students opportunities to understand wholes and parts and their relationships to each other. Students have many opportunities to discover these relationships when they work between and across the disciplines. Using interdisciplinary instruction in the two ways described above provides intellectual stimulation involving thinking, feeling, and doing behaviors that enable students to perceive ideas or concepts through different lenses that clarify or reinforce each other.

Interdisciplinary instruction stimulates learning throughout the curriculum. This instruction should be logical, occurring naturally when appropriate to the instructional aims of each arts discipline or another core subject. John Holdren, in his thoughtful essay titled "The Limits of Thematic Instruction," recommends that teachers connect disciplines when it makes sense to do so, not simply for the sake of connecting or because "everybody" is doing it.[2] When connections are carefully thought out and judiciously applied, they can be a great benefit in teaching and learning. "In the classroom, well-intentioned but overzealous attempts to interconnect everything may impede rather than advance learning. The traditional subject-matter disciplines offer concepts and categories that help us make sense of the world: boundaries can be as useful as bridges."[3]

A thoughtful curriculum design provides students with alternative ways of perceiving and experiencing the world. By discovering and using authentic connections between subjects, students can gain deeper understandings; they learn that different disciplines may look at similar issues, ideas, concepts, or events from different perspectives and apply different methodologies.

Four Components in a Comprehensive Arts Program

Each of the arts is studied from the vantage point of four dimensions: artistic perception, creative expression, historical and cultural context, and aesthetic valuing. Although each of the arts is unique, these four dimensions or components are common to the instruction of each discipline. A clear understanding of

[2] John Holdren, "The Limits of Thematic Instruction," *Common Knowledge, A Newsletter of the Core Knowledge Foundation,* Vol. 7, No. 4 (Fall, 1994).
[3] Holdren, 4.

each component is helpful when programs are evaluated for their thoroughness in the teaching of the arts.

Artistic Perception

Artistic perception, which involves processing sensory information through elements unique to the arts, sensitizes the individual to the aesthetic qualities of the world. As one develops a fuller awareness of the nuances of light, color, sound, movement, and composition through experiences in the arts, an otherwise ordinary perception takes on an artistic dimension.

Heightened artistic perception provides a stimulus for imagination and creativity and has a potential impact on all learning. The development of artistic perception enables one to comprehend and respond to the essential elements of an object or event and to express an appreciation of the work in greater depth and detail.

Artistic perception is at the heart of subject-centered instruction. Through such instruc-

tion students learn the essential vocabulary of each arts discipline and gain the basic knowledge and skills necessary to communicate in each art form.

Creative Expression

Creative expression lies in producing artworks, either by creating them or by performing the works of others. Expression in the arts includes doing the arts: learning dance styles, such as ballet, modern dance, jazz, folk, and social dancing; singing and playing instruments, alone and in ensembles; acting in plays and improvisations; creating paintings; and making ceramic pots, sculptures, and masks.

Direct, personal involvement in these expressive modes is necessary for one to understand and appreciate each discipline. Purposeful arts activities focus on, channel, and encourage communication and originality and provide increasing understanding of the structure and language of the arts. In creative expression the artistic perception appropriate to each art is embodied in concrete objects and performances.

Emphasis is placed on the process of creating as well as on the product. Creative expression is important in understanding the way in which artworks are created or performed. Creative experiences foster problem solving and reflective thinking and promote originality, imagination, and creativity.

Historical and Cultural Context

Learning the historical and cultural context of the arts leads to understanding the arts in the context of the time and place of their creation. Students studying the arts in their cultural context develop a broad understanding of the artists and performers, their works, the change in their style or emphasis over time, the effects that their society and times had on them, and the effects of their artwork on society in the past and present. Knowledge of the artistic accomplishments of great world cultures enables students to see the importance of the arts in relation to those cultures and to grasp the relevance of the arts in contemporary society. Knowledge of the arts of American and other cultures, past and present, helps students gain appreciation and understanding of those cultures and of their own personal heritage.

Students working on their own art productions or performances connect their work to that of artists in other times and places. Their research is done in libraries and museums and through slide collections, reenactments and re-creations of historic events, participation with practitioners of the arts, interviews with practicing artists and performers, and audiotaped and videotaped performances. Students gain the confidence that comes from connections with great traditions and the critical judgment that comes from considering their work along with that of their predecessors and contemporaries.

The highest purpose of art is to inspire.

—Bob Dylan, singer and songwriter

Aesthetic Valuing

Aesthetic valuing means analyzing, making informed judgments about, and pursuing meaning in the arts. It refers to a branch of philosophy called *aesthetics,* which is concerned with broad issues about the nature and components of aesthetic experience. To develop aesthetic sensibilities, students study sensory, intellectual, emotional, and philosophic bases for understanding the arts and for making judgments about their form, content, technique, and purpose. Through study, reflection, and direct experience, students develop criteria for arriving at personal judgments. They formulate a personal aesthetic, which is then applicable to a lifelong, fulfilling experience in the arts.

This process of developing judgment is the foundation of public discussion about the merit of works of creative expression. The process is commonly called criticism or the use of knowledge to assign value to a work of art. Being able to criticize justly, to value a work aesthetically, means applying knowledge of the other three components to the work being contemplated.

Three Levels of Schooling in a Comprehensive Arts Program

The vision of this edition of the *Visual and Performing Arts Framework* is that all students will experience the four components of each arts discipline during each year in a program focusing on art instruction that is (1) subject centered; (2) connected to other arts disciplines; and (3) connected to other core subjects. Successful school arts programs also provide a variety of experiences, including trips to art museums; art exhibits or festivals; and theatre, dance, and orchestra performances.

All art is the expression of one and the same thing—the relation of the spirit of man to the spirit of other men and to the world.

—Ansel Adams, photographer

Elementary School Level

Young students participate in a well-defined and carefully organized program composed of all four arts so that they develop basic knowledge and skills in dance, music, theatre, and the visual arts. Arts programs in the early grades provide students an essential first step toward developing abilities to communicate. Students gain the knowledge and skills necessary to express ideas creatively in verbal and nonverbal ways. An elementary school arts program includes doing, reading, and thinking about the arts. Instruction is delivered by a combination of specialists, generalist teachers (usually, classroom teachers in elementary school), and guest artists.

In an elementary school arts program, the arts are studied as separate disciplines and in connection with other subject areas. The inclusion and integration of all the arts with other subjects, such as mathematics, history–social science, English–language arts, and science, may require less cooperative planning in the early grades than is required at higher grade levels because one teacher generally teaches all subjects in a self-contained classroom. However, cooperation with other teachers in the same grade and across grades for the purposes of planning and team-teaching is encouraged. Integration happens more readily when the teacher is trained or has participated in comprehensive professional development to teach the knowledge and skills of the arts and make appropriate connections with other subjects.

Arts specialists at the elementary school level cooperate with classroom teachers so that students experience subject-centered curriculum in depth, with follow-up experiences. Arts curriculum and instruction are planned jointly among classroom teachers, arts specialists, and guest artists so that the classroom teacher has command of the totality of the program, can follow through, and can make further appropriate interdisciplinary connections.

Arts activities relate to the interests of the child; include products that are initiated, designed, and completed by the child; and show a balance between child-initiated and teacher-directed activities. Teachers are knowledgeable about students' artistic and aesthetic developmental stages and are respectful of children's self-expression. In addition, reading literature about the arts and artists that includes stories, biographies, and histories of dance, music, theatre, and visual arts helps students understand the connections between the work they do and creative work done by others.

In a comprehensive elementary school arts program, teachers prepare students with the knowledge and skill in all four arts to give them a foundation for further work.

Middle School Level

A middle school arts program includes all the requisites of the elementary-level program. In addition, the middle school provides individual courses in music, dance, theatre, and the visual arts to increase and refine students' knowledge and skills beyond the basics learned at the elementary level. Students experience all four arts to gain further knowledge and skills and to make personal connections with the world, the school, and themselves. Meaningful and well-planned exploration is an important part of a middle grades program. At this level talent is not an issue because knowledge and skills are still being developed. Inclusion of the four arts disciplines in an exploratory manner, common in middle school, is one way in which to expose large numbers of middle-level students to the arts. This program consists of a yearlong course for students who would not otherwise take the arts. It includes four segments, taught in rotation by specialists in dance, music, theatre, and visual arts, which continue the students' development in the four components of each art form.

The arts are often taught by separate specialists, beginning in middle school. Faculty work and plan together to offer a comprehensive arts education program for all students. Another area of collaboration is in working with visiting artists and community arts resources. It is important for faculty, artists, and the community to work together to make the arts program coherent and relevant.

High School Level

A high school arts program includes all the requisites of the elementary- and middle-level arts programs. In addition, the high school arts program supports an overall vision of secondary education, which is to engage every student in a rigorous, well-planned curriculum that enables students to make transitions from school to career. At the high school level, students continue arts courses appropriate to their long-term goals. They also continue and deepen their understanding of the arts as a way of appreciating, experiencing, and valuing the world. During their high school years, students have the opportunity to continue with in-depth instruction in the arts by selecting at least one yearlong course in one of the four arts disciplines.

Through careful planning the problems of calendaring, daily scheduling, and cooperative curriculum planning of subject-centered as well as arts-connected instruction can be accommodated. The instruction is provided by credentialed specialists. Artists and community arts resources are important to the total program. Please refer to the section titled "Community Resources for Arts Education" in this chapter for ideas on collaborating with the arts community.

Student clubs, parent groups, and the community can enhance the curriculum by helping to create an artistically rich environment at the school, one that encourages students to develop respect and support for the arts.

Graduation and college entrance requirements often dictate the high school courses in which students elect to enroll. In many cases this process works to the disadvantage of high school courses in the arts. Students are sometimes allowed to waive arts courses in favor of another core curriculum subject. The implication is that arts courses are of lesser importance to a comprehensive education. Every consideration needs to be given to maintaining equity in access to each core subject area.

Arts for All Students in a Comprehensive Arts Program

The arts provide an avenue in which all students can work at a personalized pace, develop self-expression and self-confidence, and experience a sense of accomplishment.

Instruction in the arts allows for differences in individual learning. In the visual arts most production is individual and allows for different learning styles. In the performing arts ensembles provide opportunities for students of varied ages and expertise to succeed and to learn from each other and together. A variety of teaching strategies, both teacher directed and student centered, and various grouping strategies (individuals, pairs, small groups, and large groups) provide opportunities for all students to succeed.

All students are encouraged to participate in dance, music, theatre, and visual arts (as performers and as the audience). The advent of theatre for the deaf, wheelchair dance, museum tours for the visually impaired, and access by touch to musical sounds makes the arts more accessible. The curriculum may need modification to encourage the successful participation of students with disabilities. Any necessary modification can be discussed and coordinated with the special education staff serving those students.

Often, students learning English find their greatest fulfillment in arts classes, where their command of English and learning in other core subjects are enhanced by communication in nonverbal media. Whenever possible, instruction should be provided through the primary language and sheltered English to make the curriculum accessible to limited-English-proficient (LEP) students.[4]

Students with special needs learn, participate, and find self-expression most rewarding when the teacher prepares and implements adaptations that allow for students' individual differences and special characteristics. This is the kind of good teaching that enables all students to succeed.

Assessment in a Comprehensive Arts Program

Good assessment is good curriculum and instruction and should be embedded throughout an arts program. Curriculum-embedded

---

[4] Although some publications and individuals refer to students who are learning English as English-language learners or as English learners, this document uses the term *limited-English proficient* (LEP) because this term is the one used in law. As used in this document, LEP (limited- and non-English-speaking) students are those who do not have the clearly developed English language skills of comprehension, speaking, reading, and writing necessary to succeed in the school's regular instructional programs.

assessment identifies what students are expected to know and be able to do and how well each student achieves expectations. In conjunction with the goals set out in this framework, assessment in the arts can help raise the level of achievement of all students. An instructionally sound assessment program for the arts, established by the district and individual schools, also provides information about how to improve curriculum and instruction and increases accountability for the arts in the eyes of students, teachers, administrators, and parents.

Arts assessment in California has been pioneered by a major statewide professional initiative, the Towards Arts Assessment Project (TAAP) of the California Department of Education and the Sacramento County Office of Education. Other assessment projects have been initiated by the California Art Education Association (CAEA), the California Music Educators Association (CMEA), the California Dance Educators Association (CDEA), the California Educational Theatre Association (CETA), and The California Arts Project (TCAP). The benefits of the curriculum-embedded and performance-based assessments in the arts, as developed in the TAAP project, are described in the publication titled *Prelude to Performance Assessments in the Arts, Kindergarten Through Grade Twelve.*[5]

Assessment of student work in a comprehensive arts program may consist of the following, in any combination:

• *Portfolios.* Students at all levels keep portfolios of their work in the arts, with thoughtfully selected examples of both the process and the product. Portfolios may include productions, such as pictures, drawings, audiotapes, and videotapes; written reflections; and evidence of the students' understandings of artistic

---

[5] *Prelude to Performance Assessments in the Arts, Kindergarten Through Grade Twelve.* Sacramento: California Department of Education, 1993.

perception, historical and cultural context, and aesthetic valuing. Rubrics written to guide scoring include achievement in all four components. Rubrics may be written by teachers or by students together with teachers. They can be for student and teacher use. Rubrics can be important when communicating with parents about students' progress.

Using performance assessment is like using a magnifying glass on the students' learning. You see the learning clearly, but you don't disturb it.

—Alice Furry, Sacramento County Office of Education

Portfolios are regarded by students as their vehicle for self-assessment and reflection as well as a means of formal assessment. Students can see where they began and where they ended over a developmental period and, ultimately, should estimate their own progress.

What is a rubric?

A rubic is a scoring guide or scoring measure that is used to assess what students know and can do. A rubric defines what students are expected to achieve and has a scale of degrees of accomplishment built into it.

• *Curriculum-embedded assessments.* Assessment of student work takes place simultaneously with instruction. Portfolios are curriculum-embedded, as are group classroom projects; individual projects; journals; teacher interviews; critiques; observations; research assignments that result in written essays or class presentations; and auditions for roles in dances and plays and for chair positions in bands and orchestras. Routine instructional tasks become assessment when teachers and students reflect on the achievement of standards or expectations and evaluate and score the achievements.

- *Student performances (group or individual).* Student performances with which everyone is familiar (the choral, band, and orchestra concerts; the school play; the dance program; the art-room gallery show) become assessments when students and teachers understand the assessment process. The assessment of works in progress and of the student's progress toward a completed product are important to demonstrate student learning.[6] Student performances also provide an excellent opportunity in which to engage parents and community members in discussion and dialogue in arts programs.

- *Formal assessments (such as open-ended problems).* Some states and the National Assessment of Educational Progress (NAEP) Arts Education Assessment (which is expected to be ready for implementation in 1997) assess students'

---

[6] For a fine example of a concert used for assessment, see the contribution by Dennie Palmer Wolf and Joan B. Baron in *Measuring Up to the Challenge*. Edited by Ruth Mitchell. New York: American Council for the Arts, 1994. (Report of the American Council for the Arts symposium on assessment in the arts, held in Atlanta, September, 1992.)

responses to problems in standardized conditions; that is, students work with the same materials under the same conditions for the same amount of time in all participating schools so that meaningful comparisons can be made among arts education programs. Individual achievement is also scored and reported in meaningful ways to students, parents, and schools. Open-ended problems in the arts do not necessarily have to be answered in writing; for example, in a dance assessment students can be asked to compose and perform an original dance in response to a poem. The students' dances are videotaped for scoring at a central location.

The vision for statewide assessment in the arts in California includes assessment in each of the arts disciplines, with opportunities for students at elementary school, middle school, and high school levels to show their knowledge, skills, and abilities in all four components. Some assessment exercises are standardized, meaning that students are asked to respond to "prompts," questions, or tasks in a certain amount of time at approximately the same stage in the school year. Others are long-range, showing assessments of the process and product, and are gathered together in portfolios.

As was implied at the beginning of this section, good assessment is also good instruction. They are so intertwined that the one influences the other; often, it is not possible to identify when a student's work is being assessed and when instruction is taking place.

Community Resources for Arts Education

A comprehensive, articulated program of arts education incorporates the unique resources of the whole community. In California these resources include individual artists in each discipline; arts providers; local arts councils;

architecture; public sculpture; museums; special exhibitions; music centers; theatres; acting companies; dance companies; community orchestras; opera companies; artists' studios and cooperatives; art clubs and societies; architectural and historical societies; and businesses that support the arts. Often, dress rehearsal performances are available to students at a reduced cost. In some cities the musicians' union arranges programs for schools. And some community foundations specialize in providing arts programs for schools.

The collaborative nature of the arts is conducive to partnerships between the business community, the professional artist, the educator-artist, parents, and the school community. Partnerships provide for the sharing of resources and experiences between the ongoing curriculum or particular course of instruction and those organizations and persons outside the school.

The most memorable arts experiences for students are those that are taught by credentialed arts teachers and that involve direct contact with artists and performers, whether at the school or at a museum, studio, or performance space. A school arts liaison begins the planning process by making such contacts with the community through a representative of the local arts council or through individuals in the community who are recognized as knowledgeable about arts facilities and performances in the area. Meetings among the community contacts, the arts chairpersons, and teachers of the arts should be routine in order to plan an effective program of community arts experiences for the school—one that is aligned with and supports the kindergarten-through-grade-twelve curriculum. Community contact people know which artists and performers are available, either for guest appearances or as artists-in-residence. They know about exhibitions or festivals that are opening in the region and performances that are scheduled in theatres and concert halls. Arts chairs and faculties then decide at which points in a comprehensive arts program arts experiences most effectively enhance student learning.

Guest artists and artists-in-residence are important parts of a school's visual and performing arts program. Joint planning among community resource persons, administrators, parents, arts chairs, and teachers of the arts ensures that the program is well defined and efficiently run; for example, transportation is available for students to visit arts venues. The planners can cooperate in preparing presentations and performances that capitalize on what the students have learned and what they will experience.

Our schools must be concerned about developing the intellectual and spiritual strengths and judgments that knit together the very fabric of our society and that foster a common culture, especially in a country that prides itself on pluralism and individual freedom.

—Scott Matheson, former Governor of Utah

Joint planning should include professional development programs for both guest artists and artists-in-residence as well as the school's generalist and specialist teachers. Professional development with artists is mutually beneficial because the teachers learn about developments in the art form and the guest artists learn how to adapt their teaching to present developmentally appropriate knowledge and skills to students. Whenever possible, professional development with the guest artists should be extended to parents, school board members, administrators, and other faculty for the purpose of strengthening the program and the curriculum's connections with the arts.

Integrating outside artists into a comprehensive arts program brings the experiences of other practicing artists to the students. They see that artists are continually struggling to solve problems, to improve their skills, to focus on meaning, and to communicate effectively in their art form. Thus students begin to see themselves as members of a community of artists who inherit long-standing traditions across time and place.

Technology in the Service of the Arts

Artists in all disciplines have traditionally used and combined technologies to create and express ideas. For today's artists both known and emerging technologies are altering the direction and escalating the pace of explorations within and between arts disciplines. This change results from the easy access to vast amounts of artistic media, materials, and processes and information about historical and contemporary artists. Technological advances that provide new media, material, products, and processes for creating, displaying, and communicating aesthetic ideas are available through world-wide information technologies, such as the Internet. Electronic technologies allow communication across miles and through satellite; and make possible explorations across time, in re-creations of the past and projections into the future.

Mankind's most enduring achievement is art. At its best, it reveals the nobility that coexists in human nature along with flaws and evils, and the beauty and truth it can perceive. Whether in music or architecture, literature, painting or sculpture, art opens our eyes and ears and feelings to something beyond ourselves, something we cannot experience without the artist's vision and the genius of his craft.

—Barbara Tuchman, Pulitzer Prize-winning historian

New technologies also improve the artistic environment of schools. For example, technologies provide for safer ceramics firing procedures in ceramics classrooms, safer sound controls in music rooms, and more efficient lighting systems for stage performances.

Used appropriately, electronic technologies are magical. They extend the moment in any of the arts. For example, students performing a dance can view their performance on videotape and analyze the movement, position, and overall choreography and then create a library of improvisations or change the choreography, using a computerized dance notation program. These feedback and stop-action capabilities allow students to be inventive and take artistic risks with more confidence.

Change in teaching and learning is occurring rapidly for both teachers and students. Communities, schools, teachers, and students need to embrace new technologies as tools for the arts. Teachers are challenged to do new things with new equipment, not old things on new equipment. To adapt their knowledge, skills, and abilities, they need the opportunity to grow professionally. Allocating time for professional development in new technology is an investment not only for the arts but for all subject areas because access to information has expanded beyond the static forms of books, paintings, or songs to universal access by computer and interactive forms of communication.

Teachers can use electronic technology to enhance their teaching of the four components of each arts discipline:

Artistic perception in the arts is heightened through the use of technological tools, such as digital cameras, theatrical lighting programs, computers, and MIDIs. Opportunities for recognizing, analyzing, and synthesizing the development of skills and for observing specific techniques are exciting and meaningful.

Creative expression using new technologies is unlimited. Students and teachers incorporate new electronic technologies into lessons, presentations, and exploration in each of the arts disciplines and use the technologies in connecting the arts with other subjects in the curriculum.

Historical and cultural context is brought vividly alive with interactive software programs and access to the worldwide electronic network, the Internet. For example, on a current laser disc program, a Beethoven symphony is accompanied by pictures of the composer, his friends, and his background; copies of his original musical score; information about the instruments for which the piece was written; and information about the events that inspired the work. Similar laser discs, CD-ROM programs, and video libraries are available for dance, music, theatre, and the visual arts. Technology opens the classroom to arts of different times, places, and cultures.

Aesthetic valuing is supported by both old and new technologies, which offer a range of choices for students' reflection on and evaluation of the arts. From written reflection to multimedia presentations, the use of technology provides students at all levels with an opportunity to increase the depth and breadth of their understanding of the arts.

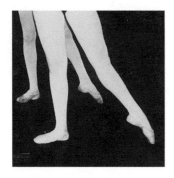

My art is just an effort to express the truth of my being in gesture and movement. From the first, I have only danced my life.

—Isadora Duncan (1877–1927)

Dance is an integral part of society. It plays a role in rite and ritual and serves social, recreational, entertainment, and artistic purposes.

Dance education integrates the students' physical and mental processes, encourages verbal responses, and promotes children's health. A comprehensive dance experience has the potential to address the development of the whole human being. As students dance, their innate creative abilities provide them with capabilities for spontaneous response and discovery of aesthetic form. When students dance with and for each other, they develop a greater respect for and understanding and appreciation of diversity.

The direct physical experience of dancing transforms the dancer into a powerful and expressive being. This transformative physical experience occurs with the dancer's mastery of each technical skill and participation in each creative act. Choreographing and performing his or her dance requires the student dancer to go beyond known experience to create new forms. Students working at this level experience exaltation, self-discovery, and enhanced self-esteem. Performing dances created by other individuals and cultures enhances the students' knowledge and understanding of others, both in the United States and in other countries, now and in other times.

Recent theories of learning lead to the view that intelligence takes many forms other than the verbal-linguistic form.[1] Dance allows students to extend their capacity for learning through these additional forms of intelligence: kinesthetic, in moving; musical, in dancing to accompaniment; spatial, in

---

[1] Howard Gardner, *Frames of Mind: The Theory of Multiple Intelligences* (Tenth anniversary edition). New York: Basic Books, Inc., 1993.

designing movement patterns; logical-mathematical, in counting, phrasing, and sequencing movement; verbal, in giving and taking instructions and feedback; intrapersonal, in sensing and using their own expressive potential; and interpersonal, in communicating and cooperating with others.

The important nonverbal experience of dance is difficult to define; yet there is general agreement that dance activity shares the following characteristics: (1) aesthetic intention, or the need to externalize an internal state (of both emotion and idea); (2) communication of nonverbal information through movement; and (3) social or ritualized interaction with others, as individuals or in groups, with audiences or partners. For the experience to qualify as a dance activity, these three characteristics must be present.

However, although such physical activities as those involved in drill team movements, gymnastics, synchronized swimming, and aerobic dance use dance-like elements, the three characteristics of dance are not central to those functions. Similarly, although dance activities involve physical training, rehearsed movement, and aspects of play, dance activities are not a part of the physical education curriculum. It is necessary for curriculum designers and administrators to keep the three characteristics of dance in mind when determining the issue of dance as related to physical education.

Students need to experience all forms of dance in a carefully structured program. These forms include creative dance, social and popular dance, and the dance of other cultures, especially of cultures related to the local community. A fully inclusive program should embrace both sexes, encourage all body types and sizes, respect ethnic diversity, and provide for students with special needs.

A dance program needs to:

1. Be well planned and developmentally appropriate, from kindergarten through grade twelve.

2. Provide opportunities for guided reflection about and analysis of dance and choreography.

3. Provide opportunities for personal skill development, with an emphasis on the creative process as well as the product.

4. Develop informed citizens with a lifelong commitment to the arts.

5. Develop students' appreciation for and understanding of the dances of many cultures and periods in world history.

At this time California does not issue a dance teaching credential. When one is available, credentialed dance specialists and trained generalists will be able to offer a comprehensive dance program. For now the dance specialist, artist in residence, or district dance and movement specialist needs to collaborate with the district curriculum specialist and the classroom teacher to design an effective dance curriculum.

The Four Components of Dance Education

The dance activities identified in the goals on pages 42–47 align with the four components of dance education as well as with the motor, social-emotional, and cognitive developmental levels of the students in each grade range. Students who have had little or no dance experience or instruction should master the concepts in the preceding level before attempting those suggested for their own grade level.

I see the dance being used as a means of communication between soul and soul— to express what is too deep, too fine for words.

—Ruth St. Denis (1878–1968)

Artistic Perception

Artistic perception encompasses the physical experience of dance technique and improvisation. Students discover and learn dance vocabulary through the physical experience of the dance elements of time, space, and force. They develop kinesthetic awareness, movement communication skills, capacity for movement response, and motor efficiency through multisensory activities. Inherent in this component is appreciation for one's own and others' unique ways of moving. Students learn to respect the unique strengths and weaknesses of different body types, weights, and sizes. They confront the notion that dance is an art form designed for a specific body type and understand that dance is accessible to all students.

Creative Expression

In dance as a creative experience, the student uses intuition as a source of movement and inspiration. The experience of improvising and forming movement patterns and compositions leads to the discovery of one's ability to create authentic dance forms. Personal creativity in dance is developed as students explore movement in both spontaneous and structured assignments. As students learn to express feelings and ideas through movement, they grow in their abilities and begin to develop original compositions. They learn to appreciate and care for their bodies through proper conditioning, dance technique, rest, and nutrition. Mutual respect and appreciation for the uniqueness of each individual's expression are developed through shared experiences.

In addition, many cultures have long traditions of formal dance performance. In Europe, for example, dances for the court were prescribed by tradition and the particular royalty for which they were performed. In the United States many forms of modern dance have evolved from very different sources but in many ways are as prescribed by their sources and influences as those found in Europe. Students need to be able to understand and perform in formal or ritualized dance as well as to create their own personal dance experience.

Historical and Cultural Context

The deep and complex heritage of dance tradition is derived from the contributions of all cultural groups, past and present. An understanding of dance history helps students recognize and appreciate the cultural differences and commonalities that make up the pluralistic human experience. The study of historical, cultural, social, and contemporary expressions of dance uncovers the influences of one cultural style on another. As students are given opportunities to share personal cultural experiences and ideas, elements of individual traditions are connected with elements of shared cultures. Dance students are able to view historical and cultural concepts, events, and themes from the perspectives of diverse contexts.

Aesthetic Valuing

Aesthetic valuing enables students to make critical judgments about the quality and success of a dance composition and performance from their own experiences and perceptions in dance. Students reveal their opinions and newly acquired knowledge through both oral and written analyses. Criteria for making critical judgments emerge from discussions between students and teachers, often using professional examples and expert opinion as a guide. Before viewing a dance performance in class, on video, or at a live concert, students learn to describe, with reasoning, their aesthetic choices and the standards that they have developed through experience and discussion.

Curriculum and Instruction in Dance Education

Because dance is both a physical discipline and a performing art, it is offered at the elementary school level as a part of regular classroom experiences. At the middle school and high school levels, the dance program is offered in a visual and performing arts department. Each school should employ at least one dance teacher who is trained in and knowledgeable about teaching the knowledge, skills, and art of dance.

Dance is concerned with the single instant as it comes along.

—Merce Cunningham (1922–)

Elementary School

All students in California elementary schools need to be engaged in dance activities as a part of their regular classroom experiences. Whenever possible, the classroom teacher should participate in planning and carrying out the dance program.

Students in elementary schools are able to identify and experience a variety of dance forms. They are introduced to the vocabulary of dance used in a discussion of a dance performance. Instruction is also focused on

helping students understand the historical and cultural contexts of dance forms, styles, and group expressions.

Through an emphasis on creative process as well as on final performance, the elementary school dance curriculum provides opportunities for students to accept their own creative potential and be open to their own original expressions. This ability, in turn, can lead to an acceptance of the work of others.

The elementary school dance program provides opportunities for young dancers to explore and experience a variety of dance forms through the four components described in this framework. Schools should provide instruction and presentation materials, including films, audio- and videotapes, prints, photographs, rhythm instruments, and literature on dance, that are appropriate for elementary school students. Exposing students to a variety of experiences in dance provides them with opportunities to define personal and cultural understandings and insights as well as develop dance knowledge and skills.

Middle School

The middle school dance program extends the elementary school learning and experiences in dance. A comprehensive middle school dance curriculum enables middle-grade students to acquire knowledge of dance, develop dance skills, and expand their creative potential in dance. It encourages students to continue a lifelong involvement in and appreciation of dance in its many forms.

Instruction in the middle school heightens the students' perceptual awareness of the aesthetic qualities of the world environment and in major works of dance. Students develop observational skills, acquire knowledge of the natural and human-made environment, and become perceptive and observant. Middle school dance programs provide opportunities for students to apply the elements of dance and extend their knowledge of the language of dance and ability to use it in both verbal and nonverbal ways.

Students explore the creative process through their own dance compositions and expressions, translating ideas, thoughts, and feelings into original pieces of choreography. They also study dance forms from many cultures and time periods in the cultural and historical context of their creation. Students develop the skills for making aesthetic judgments and engaging in thoughtful reasoning for those judgments.

High School

The high school dance program should be an integral part of the school's visual and performing arts department. A high school dance curriculum provides opportunities for students to begin in-depth studies in one or more areas of concentration.

Instruction at the high school level provides a variety of learning opportunities in dance in which students learn the language of dance and move into innovative and challenging experiences. Creative thinking in the four

Dance Across the Curriculum

As Jill Beck reports in the journal *On Common Ground*, the Dance Division at Southern Methodist University is collaborating with a school in the Dallas/Fort Worth area to link a variety of disciplines with arts education. In one of the links, after-school programs were designed with area teachers for grades 4–6 to integrate dance study with practice in abilities measured on the yearly state test and endorsed in the National Standards for Arts in Education. For example, students studying geography read maps to locate places and patterns of human migration. They learn to apply such spatial concepts as counterclockwise, asymmetrical, and the four cardinal directions. They memorize existing dances and create original dances, using these spatial concepts and embedding them with their own intent and meaning. They document their dances in the symbolic language of dance notation, perform their dances for their families and teachers, and talk about mapmaking and geography, becoming increasingly comfortable with speaking, explaining, dancing, and problem solving in public.

Jill Beck, "Partnering University Dance and the Schools: Toward the Vertical Integration of Education," *On Common Ground* (Fall, 1995), 18.

components of dance education should be promoted through a sequence of appropriate introductory, intermediate, and advanced dance courses.

Connections of dance to other curriculum areas expand and enhance the scope of the student's educational experience.

Students with Special Needs

The significance of the dance experience for students with special needs is not the degree of technical expertise they achieve but the success they enjoy in reaching their greatest potential. Students with special needs of all kinds benefit socially from their interactions with students in mainstream classes. Adaptations and modifications in instruction may be necessary to accommodate students' language, physical, and educational needs and should be supported by resource personnel. For example, students confined to a wheelchair can move one or more body parts and move in their chairs independently or with the help of other students. Students with physical disabilities can work collaboratively with others to choreograph dances that incorporate the use of the wheelchair or involve the stationary mover.

Dance programs in elementary, middle, and high schools can provide students at risk of dropping out with the needed incentive to stay in school. These students may find a sense of connection and community in the dance class, overcome their feelings of alienation, and identify connections with other core subjects that increase their interest in school.

Students with limited English proficiency and those who speak English as a second language also benefit greatly from a dance program. They are integrated readily into dance classes because communication occurs through physical demonstration of concepts and repetition of activities. For example,

through a visual demonstration of improvisation involving simple shape elements, these students can successfully experience basic design elements. Because dance has a language of its own, every participant learns the language on an equal basis.

Students with obvious natural talent as dancers, performers, or choreographers require support and encouragement to enhance their gifts. At the same time teachers need to provide the students with a balanced program and allow them to grow in the skill areas that do not come as easily to them. The multiple roles in dance allow all students to succeed.

Student Performances

Inventive and careful planning allows beginning performing experiences to be shared experiences rather than "show" activities that exploit students and distort the educational dance program. Planned performances, an outgrowth of the students' capacity to move

expressively at levels compatible with their age and physical ability, avoid the tendency to produce high-powered performances with a few select students. The dance material is appropriate for the level, skills, learning situation, knowledge, and understanding of both the participants and the audience.

At first the performances provide for informal presentations in the classroom or studio. Student performers share a newly acquired skill, demonstrate their solution to a problem, or evaluate a particular experience in dance. The next step provides for more formal dance presentations as students become more skilled and the performances involve the expertise of the other arts.

The visibility and popularity of student performing groups may, however, result in performance expectations not directly related to dance education. Demands are often made on school dance groups to perform at athletic events, assemblies, student productions, parent meetings, community clubs, conferences, and civic events. Providing entertainment may be a valid activity of performance groups but should never interfere with the students' dance education.

Assessment in Dance Education

Assessment in dance focuses students' and teachers' attention on the inseparability of assessment and instruction. As indicated in Chapter 2, assessment becomes instruction when students and teachers reflect together on content standards or expectations of achievement and discuss ways of achieving those standards.

Wolf and Pistone enumerate five assumptions about the efficacy of assessment in the arts. First, both students and teachers insist on excellence of learning, as exhibited in performance. High standards are set, and rehearsals and discussion involve ways in which to reach those standards. Second, there is much talk about judgment—opinions on a range of qualitative issues—and decisions based on insight, reason, and craft. Third, self-assessment is important for all artists and performers. Students need to learn how to understand and appraise their own work as well as that of their peers and other dancers and choreographers. Fourth, varied forms of assessment need to be utilized to obtain information about both individual and group performances. These forms are discussed in Chapter 2 and include everyday conversation and comments, critiques, and reviews. Fifth, continuous assessment allows students to reflect on their own performance and use the insights gained from this process to enrich their work. Viewed in this way, assessment is an episode of learning.[2]

Wolf and her colleagues, who developed the handbook titled *Arts Propel: A Handbook for Music,* make an assumption that "ongoing assessment, both formal and informal, by students themselves and by teachers (in effect a dialogue about work and ways of working), yields revealing profiles of

[2] D. P. Wolf and N. Pistone, *Taking Full Measure: Rethinking Assessment Through the Arts.* New York: College Entrance Examination Board, 1991.

development and promotes learning and new levels of achievement."[3]

The following example illustrates the way in which assessment directs student effort so that the result is satisfying to the teacher and student alike:

In high school advanced dance students participated in an assessment project involving portfolio and performance components. Early in the year students elected to improve their choreographic skills and collaborated with the teacher to develop scoring criteria for the project. The selection of criteria was based on elements of good choreography, such as the use of contrast, levels, and unity. The students were not restricted in making creative choices but had to justify their music selections in relation to the intent for their piece. They were also required to maintain a written record of their thoughts about the choreographic process. Midway through the semester students were evaluated by their peers and the teacher, who used the rubric developed earlier in the year. They then reworked their pieces for a final evaluation at the end of the year. This assignment turned out so successfully that many of the pieces were performed in a formal concert for the public.

The Role of Technology in Dance Education

Although the technology for dance classes is in a formative stage, video and computer technologies do offer effective instruments that should be considered in developing instructional strategies.

---

[3] *Arts Propel: A Handbook for Music.* Edited by Ellen Winner. Cambridge, Mass.: Educational Testing Service and Harvard Project Zero, 1992.

Video technology allows the dance student to view videotapes containing a variety of historical, cultural, and biographical information on dance. CD-ROMs help students create multimedia images and text. These electronic tools can provide optimum teaching effectiveness and enhance student achievement.

The student can also instantly record movement improvisations and create a library from which original dances can be choreographed. A dance notation system that uses computer-generated graphics and text overlaid on videotape assists the student with musical counts, spatial positioning, and verbal descriptions of movement qualities.

In addition, these technologies can change the teacher's method of time management and the student's self-assessment process. In dance classes the instructor demonstrates movement patterns and reinforces the learning process by providing imagery and corrections. Video and computer technologies now enable students to see directly what a particular movement looks like, a process that enhances their understanding and helps perfect their performance.

Teacher Preparation and Professional Development

Teachers are best prepared to teach dance when they have majored in dance in their college or university undergraduate program. In addition, the inclusion of dance in the core of courses required for single-subject and multiple-subjects credentials in colleges and universities helps prepare all teachers to teach the knowledge and skills of dance. Prospective teachers need to understand the processes of learning and strategies of instruction appropriate to the ages and abilities of students. Teachers of dance need to have the same academic preparation in their discipline as do teachers in other core disciplines.

School districts are encouraged to support dance specialists and to provide for teachers' continual professional growth in dance. Teachers need to be encouraged to enroll in dance courses in local colleges and universities and be allowed opportunities to participate in special workshops offered by professional dance organizations.

There's only one of me. There's only one of anybody. That's why steps look different on different people.

—Judith Jamison (1944–)

Dance teachers or generalists in kindergarten through grade six need to be able to provide an environment that fosters students' love of movement. This objective can be achieved principally when teachers know and teach the basic elements of the dance and movement medium, including social and cultural dance forms. In addition, teachers need to know how to lead students in expressing and experiencing dance through structured improvisation and creative problem solving.

Dance teachers at the middle and high school levels should be able to structure and teach specialized dance technique classes appropriate to students' skill levels, needs, and interests. Those teachers also must be able to recognize talented dance students and challenge them to expand their talents by referring the students to other special learning environments and opportunities.

Professional development can occur through workshops, demonstrations, or exchanged classroom visits with peers; coaching or mentoring by district and county office specialists; courses at institutions of higher education; participation in meetings and conferences of state and national arts and educational professional organizations; and

such institutes and workshops as those offered by The California Arts Project (TCAP).

A rapidly expanding area of dance is dance science. It includes dance medicine (care and prevention of injuries); biomechanical, physiological issues in dance; nutritional concerns; and body therapies. Teachers who are aware of the integration of scientific concepts of human movement into traditional dance teaching methods can help students understand that they are athletes as well as artists. Teachers' training methods should stem from sound principles of kinesiology, nutrition, and preventive injury training.

Resources, Environment, Materials, and Equipment

A quality dance program needs special materials and equipment and a special location. Adequate open, cleared floor space must be provided. However, every program in dance has its own distinct characteristics and must tailor its program to a given set of circumstances.

Safety must be considered. A resilient wood floor is particularly important because injuries occur easily on hard or cement surfaces. The ceiling needs to be of sufficient height to accommodate adagio work at the secondary level. Rooms need to be well ventilated, with a heating and cooling system that can be adjusted to make the room comfortable for dancers. If the room is large enough for collapsible benches at one end, the space can be used for demonstrations and performances.

Storage space is needed for materials and equipment, and, at the secondary level, space for dressing is needed.

Dance classes need some or all of the following materials and equipment:

1. *Musical accompaniment.* Percussion instruments are essential to any creative

movement class and are used for rhythmic training, with locomotor activities, and for student dance compositions. A single-headed, tunable dance drum, sometimes called a *Wigman* drum, played with a lamb's wool beater or with the hand, and a single or double bongo drum played with the hand are two excellent possibilities. Also recommended is a set of three single-headed plastic drums that possess pleasing timbre and are light and easy to carry.

In addition to a satisfactory hand drum, other percussion instruments provide accompanying sounds that vary in tone, timbre, duration, and intensity.

A piano is standard equipment in most dance studios. Even a teacher without a regular accompanist can use the piano when students are working on movement qualities, rhythmic materials, and phrasing.

Additional material and equipment needs include multiple-speed compact-disc or tape players, a video camera and playback equipment, and body mats for improvisation.

2. *Materials for costumes and props.* Materials that are useful for improvisation and composition work include scarves, streamers, balls, balloons, paper bags, newspapers, ropes, elastics, costume items (e.g., hats, capes, skirts, jackets), crayons, paper, pieces of fabric, and masks.

Excellence in dance instruction supersedes in importance any resources, materials, or equipment. When powerful teaching and learning occur, teaching aids enhance the experience of the learner and enrich each student's dance experience. Materials and equipment are secondary to the interaction between a teacher and a student.

Goals for Dance Education

Artistic Perception Component

Goal 1. *Students develop body awareness; movement communication skills; and a capacity for movement response, motor efficiency, and multisensory integration.*

Goal 2. *Students explore dance elements and perform dance movements, using the skills, vocabulary, and language of dance.*

Creative Expression Component

Goal 3. *Students make connections between dance composition and performance and healthful living.*

Goal 4. *Students use choreographic principles and processes to express perceptions, feelings, images, and thoughts.*

Goal 5. *Students create and communicate meaning through dance composition and performance.*

Historical and Cultural Context Component

Goal 6. *Students develop knowledge and understanding of human diversity through dance.*

Goal 7. *Students investigate the role of dance in historical and contemporary cultures.*

Aesthetic Valuing Component

Goal 8. *Students analyze, interpret, and judge dance in accord with learned aesthetic principles.*

Artistic Perception Component

Goal 1. *Students develop body awareness; movement communication skills; and a capacity for movement response, motor efficiency, and multisensory integration.*

Examples of Knowledge and Skills for Goal 1

Kindergarten Through Grade Four	Grades Five Through Eight	Grades Nine Through Twelve Proficient	Grades Nine Through Twelve Advanced
Students respond spontaneously in movement to various stimuli: sounds, music, colors, textures, objects, imagery, and feelings.	Students focus attention on kinesthetic awareness in responding to a variety of stimuli and perform specific and repeatable movement sequences taught by the instructor.	Students consistently respond from the center of the body to various stimuli and perform movement sequences of increasing complexity, which are taught by the instructor.	Students use technical skills to express movement that is increasingly clearer and deeper in emotional tone, dramatic intent, and artistic style.
Students verbally describe how movement feels, using basic dance vocabulary.	Students verbally or through written journals describe movement and movement choices, using dance vocabulary.	Students observe dances and discuss dance movement elements and choices from a kinesthetic perspective, using appropriate dance terminology.	Student dancers demonstrate kinesthetic awareness and critical understanding in verbal and written analyses of specific dances. Student responses include references to other art forms, dance history, politics, and so forth.
Students discover movements they like to perform.	Students expand their preferred movement choices, developing greater strength, flexibility, and motor control.	Students demonstrate ability to perform the dance movements of their peers with technical accuracy and clarity of emotional or dramatic intent.	Students learn the dances of professionals and expand their natural inclinations and learned technical skills to include ranges of movement that challenge their safety zones.

Goal 2. *Students explore dance elements and perform dance movements, using the skills, vocabulary, and language of dance.*

Examples of Knowledge and Skills for Goal 2

Students demonstrate spatial concepts through movement (e.g., personal and general spaces; shapes at different levels; shapes of different sizes; and curved and straight pathways).	Students demonstrate an understanding of spatial elements, using axial and locomotor movements.	Students identify and perform long and complex phrases and patterns from two different traditions and types of dance.	Student dancers demonstrate deep understanding of the use of space by choreographing a dance work, using the spatial ideas of a master choreographer.

Examples of Knowledge and Skills for Goal 2 *(Continued)*

Kindergarten Through Grade Four	Grades Five Through Eight	Grades Nine Through Twelve Proficient	Grades Nine Through Twelve Advanced
Students demonstrate the concepts of time through movement activities (e.g., pulse, tempo, and rhythm) and relate these time experiences to their own breath and heartbeat.	Students demonstrate ability to perceive and move to varying musical beats and rhythms.	Students create and perform combinations and variations, using meters (5/4, 11/8), and compose phrases and dances that change meter and rhythmic patterns.	Student dancers perform dances with interpretive musicality and correctness; handle polyrhythms in their own bodies with confidence; and dance musically, with or without accompaniment.
Students demonstrate concepts of force (e.g., heavy/light and percussive/sustained).	Students demonstrate understanding of and ability to manipulate forces and qualities of movement.	Students create and perform combinations and variations, using the full range of the elements of space, time, and force.	Students perform dances projecting artistic expression, clarity, musicality, and stylistic nuance.

Creative Expression Component

 Goal 3. *Students make connections between dance composition and performance and healthful living.*

Examples of Knowledge and Skills for Goal 3

Kindergarten Through Grade Four	Grades Five Through Eight	Grades Nine Through Twelve Proficient	Grades Nine Through Twelve Advanced
Students understand how healthy practices (e.g., good nutrition and adequate rest) enhance the ability to dance.	Students create warm-up exercises and explain how they prepare the body and mind for expressive purposes in dance.	Students lead warm-up exercises that are safe and designed for a variety of body types.	Student dancers demonstrate ability to correct standard techniques to prevent injury.
Students describe how to protect the body from physical injuries.	Through demonstration or performance students describe strategies for the prevention of dance injuries.	Students monitor growth in skill development and performance ability in regular written or performance analyses, which emphasize anatomy and physical challenges.	Student dancers use written or performance analyses of skill and performance level to set new physical self-challenges.

Goal 4. *Students use choreographic principles and processes to express perceptions, feelings, images, and thoughts.*

Examples of Knowledge and Skills for Goal 4

Kindergarten Through Grade Four	Grades Five Through Eight	Grades Nine Through Twelve Proficient	Grades Nine Through Twelve Advanced
Students improvise dances based on a variety of auditory, motor, visual, and tactile stimuli, emotional states, ideas, textures, shapes, and concepts.	Students transform movement from pantomimic representation to abstract illusion and imagery.	Students organize improvisational ideas into the choreography of dances that demonstrate clarity of intent, unity, originality, and coherent form.	Student dancers research a theme; then prepare a storyboard, compose a five-minute dance, and write program notes based on the dance theme.
Students originate simple rhythm patterns in sound and movement based on rhythms of their own bodies, a clock, and the ocean.	Students translate aural rhythmic patterns and sequences into movement.	Students identify and perform the vocabulary of time in relation to dance: accelerate, decelerate, legato, adagio, and syncopation.	Student dancers demonstrate rhythmic acuity and musicality in composing three dances, each demonstrating a particular use of music (e.g., syncopation, tone color, mixed meter).

 Goal 5. *Students create and communicate meaning through dance composition and performance.*

Examples of Knowledge and Skills for Goal 5

Students create a sequence of simple movements from the movements of a real-life event, such as an event in nature at a park, a snowball fight, or someone running from a dog.	Students choreograph dance studies based on a theme that has personal meaning or significance.	Students create dances based on contemporary social themes and discuss the relationship of expressive movement, motifs, phrases, and dance compositions to meaning.	Student dancers compare and contrast, through class discussion, the way in which meaning is communicated in two student-choreographed works and two professional works with similar themes.
Students perform dance sequences for classmates and describe how different tempos make them feel different.	Students demonstrate ability to rework dances as a result of class discussion and self-evaluation. After hearing peer responses to their dance study, students rework that study.	Using the aesthetic language of dance, students formulate and answer questions about the way in which specific movement choices communicate abstract ideas.	Student dancers examine the ways in which a dance creates and conveys meaning by considering the dance from a variety of cultural perspectives.

Historical and Cultural Context Component

Goal 6. *Students develop knowledge and understanding of human diversity through dance.*

Examples of Knowledge and Skills for Goal 6

Kindergarten Through Grade Four	Grades Five Through Eight	Grades Nine Through Twelve Proficient	Grades Nine Through Twelve Advanced
Students learn and perform folk, historical, cultural, and contemporary dances.	Students identify and discuss commonalities, such as costume, gesture, rhythmic structure, music, and form of dance, in historical, cultural, and contemporary forms and types of dance.	Students re-create historical, cultural, and contemporary dance styles and forms after viewing them on film, video, or computer notation.	Student dancers explore and discuss why and how people dance and how dance reflects basic beliefs and changes in society, especially in social, leisure, and health activities.
Students learn and perform a dance from their own or another culture.	Students learn and perform dances from their own or another culture and teach them to others.	Students perform complex folk, historical, cultural, and contemporary dances from their own and others' cultures.	Student dancers review videotapes, films, or computer notations of various historical, cultural, and contemporary dance styles and forms and write analyses of their cultural commonalities.

Goal 7. *Students investigate the role of dance in historical and contemporary cultures.*

Examples of Knowledge and Skills for Goal 7

Students observe historical and contemporary dance performances and participate in a conversation with the dancers.	Students observe and analyze cultural commonalities in contemporary dance styles and forms.	Students observe and discuss the effects of technology on contemporary dance styles and forms.	Student dancers perform and videotape their performance for discussion and oral and written analyses of the significance of their own dance as a contemporary cultural expression. Students hypothesize about and compare and contrast the ways in which the work might have been different if it had been created by their parents, grandparents, forefathers, and foremothers.

Examples of Knowledge and Skills for Goal 7 *(Continued)*

Kindergarten Through Grade Four	Grades Five Through Eight	Grades Nine Through Twelve Proficient	Grades Nine Through Twelve Advanced
Students watch a video of a historical dance form and describe what they see and feel.	Students observe and discuss historical dance styles and forms in performance and on film, video, and computer notation.	Students analyze the influence of cultural dance styles and forms on historical dance.	Student dancers research historical dance styles and forms in relation to social, political, economic, and technological forces and choreograph a dance based on those styles and forms.

Aesthetic Valuing Component

 Goal 8. *Students analyze, interpret, and judge dance in accord with learned aesthetic principles.*

Examples of Knowledge and Skills for Goal 8

Students explore, discover, and appreciate multiple solutions to simple given and self-discovered movement problems; choose one solution; and discuss reasons for the choice.	Students create a dance study and three variations, watch the variations on video, and select the preferred variation. Students perform the preferred variation and discuss reasons for their choice.	Students create a dance and revise it over time, articulate the reasons for their artistic decisions, and analyze the developments from those decisions.	Student dancers refine a self-choreographed dance and analyze in writing their artistic decisions and the resulting developments.
Students observe two simple dances and discuss the similarities and differences in the use of one or more of the dance elements (space, time, energy/force).	Students identify aesthetic criteria and use those criteria as a basis for the evaluation of observed dances.	Students establish a set of aesthetic criteria, based on their own preferences and the parameters of established dance criticism, and apply them both verbally and in writing in evaluations of their own and others' work.	Student dancers research the aesthetic criteria applied to different forms of dance in different cultures, noting how the criteria compare and contrast with their personal aesthetic. Students note their preferences and biases. They watch a dance from another historical period or culture and write a response from the standpoint of a visiting reporter who has arrived on the scene.

Glossary: The Language of Dance

abstraction. An idea or concept, conveyed through movement, that is removed from its original context. For example, when a gesture, such as jumping to communicate happiness, is enlarged, made polyrhythmic, and repeated on different levels, it becomes abstract, nonliteral. The use of abstraction has the potential to encourage originality and to make movement interesting and engaging.

axial movement. Nonlocomotor (stationary) movement of body parts around the axis of the body. Bending, twisting, reaching, pivoting, hand waving, and leg kicks are selected examples of axial movement.

ballet. A classical Western dance form that originated in the Renaissance courts of Europe. By the time of Louis XIV (mid-1600s), steps and body positions underwent codification. The Romantic ballet, as it is known today, began and flourished in the 1800s, led by Jules Perrot in France, August Bournonville in Denmark, and Marius Petipa in Russia. Further development of this type of dance was the work of Michel Fokine (Russia); Kenneth MacMillan and Anthony Tudor (England); and George Balanchine, Jerome Robbins, and Arthur Mitchell (United States).

choreography. The art of composing dances, including shaping movement, structuring phrases, and revising and refining dances.

creative movement, creative dance. Dance based on improvisation; the free exploration of movement, usually stimulated by an emotional or narrative theme (e.g., anger, war), or the exploration of a movement element—time, force, or space (e.g., finding ways of moving on various levels or with varying amounts or qualities of force [energy]).

a dance. A unified work, similar to a poem, a piece of music, a play, or a painting. Its structure has a beginning, middle, and end; it is unified by a purpose or set of movement themes into a recognized form. It is often rhythmic or accompanied by music.

dance. The field of study, including the functions of dance in society in the past and present and methods of choreography and performance. Dance includes kinesiology, dance therapy, dance education, dance medicine, and other related studies.

dance for children, or movement exploration. The basis of dances for expressive and imaginative purposes in which no set movements are used from an established dance technique, such as those in ballet, modern, or jazz.

dance form. Organization of dance elements into patterns, such as call-response-call (ABA), chorus-verse, or canon. The term is often confused with types of dance, such as ballet, modern, jazz.

dance medium. Body movement as the material of dance, as sound is the medium of music. The elements of dance are space, time, and force.

dance notation. Various systems of writing and recording dance movements. Most frequently used systems include Benesh notation and Laban notation. Late twentieth-century technology has made the use of the videotape an indispensable method of recording dance.

dance phrase. A partial dance idea composed of a series of connecting movements, similar to a sentence in the written form.

dance study. Usually, a minute or two of exploration of a particular dance theme or problem; it may be improvised or composed.

dance style. An individual performer's way of performing any kind of dance, such as ballet, modern, or jazz; a school of dance, such as Vaganova in Russia or Royal Academy of Dance in England; reference to a historical period, such as the Romantic period of ballet (1880s) or early modern dance (1900 to 1940).

dance type or kind (genre). Frequently confused with form and style. Examples of genre are ballet, modern, tap, jazz, Indonesian, East Indian, Bugaku. Each kind of dance is characterized by a recognizable technique, system, vocabulary of movement, composition form, and way of performing.

Dunham technique. A type of dance created by Katherine Dunham that fuses African-Haitian dance, ballet, and modern and jazz dance types.

elements of dance. The sensory components used to create and talk about dance. The components are *force, space,* and *time* (see individual entries in alphabetical order).

entertainment or commercial dance. A type of dance—often employing jazz, tap, ballet, and modern dance—employed in Broadway musicals, film, television, and music videos. Choreographers such as Agnes de Mille, Jerome Robbins, Michael Kidd, Janet Jackson, Michael Jackson, and Debbie Allen have brought life to this truly American type of dance.

folk dance. The dance associated with a national purpose. Today, it is usually performed as a surviving portion of a traditional celebration.

force. This element is characterized by the release of potential energy into kinetic energy. It utilizes body weight, reveals the effects of gravity on the body, is projected into space, and affects emotional and spatial relationships and intentions. The most recognized qualities of movement (ways in which to release energy) are sustained, percussive, suspended, swinging, and collapsing.

improvisation. Movement generated without previous planning; impromptu.

jazz dance. Dance marked by movement isolations and complex, propulsive polyrhythms. Jazz dance was an outgrowth of African American ragtime, jazz, spirituals, blues, work songs, and so forth. This type of dance was also influenced by East Indian, Gypsy, Spanish, Caribbean, and South American gestures and rhythms. Jazz dance was further explored by choreographers Lester Wilson, Jack Cole, and Bob Fosse.

kinesthetic awareness. Conscious perception of movement. Kinesthetic awareness is developed and enhanced in dance education.

locomotor movement. The movement of the body through space. It may be categorized as steps: *walk, run, hop, jump, leap, skip, slide, gallop.* When it is categorized as movement, it includes *creep, crawl, scoot,* and so forth.

modern dance. A type of dance that began as a rebellion against steps and positions and valued expressive and original or authentic movement. It is a twentieth-century idiom, first explored by American Isadora Duncan throughout Europe and by Mary Wigman and Rudolph Laban in Germany. Other significant innovators in the United States were Ruth St. Denis, Ted Shawn, Martha Graham, Doris Humphrey, and Charles Weidman, who are considered to be the pioneers of modern dance.

motif. A distinctive and recurring gesture used for thematic purposes and to unify ideas.

popular. Contemporary dance prevalent at any one time, such as the jitterbug, twist, or hip-hop.

postmodern dance. A type of dance, introduced by Merce Cunningham, which emerged in the 1960s and is generally characterized by a departure from narrative theme and evocative emotion. The use of pedestrian gesture and minimalism is characteristic of this type of dance; it is exemplified by Yvonne Ranier, Trisha Brown, Steve Paxton, and Rudy Perez.

rhythm. The organization or pattern of pulses or beats. It may be metered or unmetered and may involve music or the sounds made by the human body (such as foot stomps, heartbeats, breath).

ritual dance. A type of dance associated with spiritual ceremonies or rites of passage in a particular culture.

shape. An aspect of space that is an inherent part of locomotor and nonlocomotor movement. Shape involves the line of the body. It can be symmetrical or asymmetrical, open or closed, jagged or smooth.

social dance. A dance usually done with a partner, including ballroom and other dances for couples.

space. As an element of dance, the immediate, spherical space surrounding the body in all directions. Use of space includes shape, direction, path, range, and level of movement. Space is also the location of a performed dance—where dance takes place.

tap dance. A type of dance that concentrates on footwork and rhythm. This type of dance grew out of American popular dancing, with significant roots in African American, Irish, and English clogging traditions. Bill "Bojangles" Robinson, Eddie Rector, John Bubbles, Gregory Hines, Honi Coles, Fred Astaire, Eleanor Powell, and Gene Kelly have been landmark performers and choreographers of tap dancing.

technique. The physical skills essential to the performer; the training of the dancer for dancing.

time. An element of dance involving rhythm, phrasing, tempo, accent, duration. Time can be metered, as in music, or it can be based on body rhythms, such as breath and heartbeat.

transition. The bridging point at which a single movement, the end of a phrase, or even the end of a larger section of a dance sequences into the next movement, phrase, or section of dance.

Chapter 4

Music

Music can name the unnamable and communicate the unknowable.

—Leonard Bernstein (1918–1994)

The myths and religions of many cultures depict music as a gift of divine origin. The word *music* comes from the Greek *Muse,* any of the nine sister goddesses who reigned over the arts and sciences in Greek mythology. Existing in every culture and generation, music embodies the distinctly human need to organize sounds to express the dimensions of human feeling.

Music is a powerful manifestation of cultural heritage. It occurs in a wide variety of styles and types in cultures around the world. Studying music helps students learn about the traditions and modes of thought of their native cultures as well as those of other cultures. Because music can promote harmony between cultures in a pluralistic society, mutual cross-cultural understanding is a goal of music education.

Music is an extensive field of study, with its own body of knowledge, skills, and ways of thinking and perceiving. Recent theories lead to the view that musical intelligence is a form of intelligence, included in those described by Gardner, that is distinct from verbal-linguistic and other intelligences.[1] Musical thought and comprehension involve the mental processing of tonal-rhythmic patterns in order to make decisions about the music that is heard, performed, or created.[2]

Music provides a means for creativity and self-expression. Young students learn that their thoughts and feelings can be communicated nonverbally through music. More mature students compose and improvise original music that involves higher-order

[1] Howard Gardner, *Frames of Mind: The Theory of Multiple Intelligences* (Tenth anniversary edition). New York: Basic Books, Inc., 1993.

[2] Mary L. Serafine, *Music as Cognition.* New York: Columbia University Press, 1988.

thinking processes, such as those involved in skill mastery, analysis, and synthesis.

Music provides opportunities for success and engages the imagination of students who may have difficulty with other aspects of the curriculum. The art of music inspires students to become sensitive listeners, able to make aesthetic judgments and appreciate the essential nature of music.

Listening to the works of master composers, studying the influence of society on a composer's works and the composer's influence on society, and conducting research about comparative and contrasting aspects of music around the world enable students to use their curiosity, imagination, and intellect.

A music program needs to:

1. Be well planned and developmentally appropriate, from kindergarten through grade twelve.

2. Provide opportunities for guided reflection about and analysis of music, both written and heard.

3. Provide opportunities for personal skill development, with emphasis on the creative process as well as the product.

4. Develop informed citizens with a lifelong commitment to the arts.

5. Develop students' appreciation for and understanding of the music of many cultures and periods in world history.

The Four Components of Music Education

Effective music instruction incorporates all four arts components: artistic perception, creative expression, historical and cultural context, and aesthetic valuing. An effective teacher of music understands that students need to listen carefully, perceive patterns, and understand the use of the elements of music in performing and creating music.

Artistic Perception

Artistic perception in music is a complex activity that includes listening, contemplating, analyzing, evaluating, and feeling. Aural perception is a part of all musical activities. The teacher's task is to enhance students' sensitivity to the elements and principles of music. Although musical perception begins with exposure to music, it is developed through critical listening. The perception of sound and sound patterns is the first step in musical learning. The learner then develops concepts and understandings about music that are based on perceptions.

Students listen to and analyze music of various cultures while they develop their ability to recognize and understand the elements of music: melody, harmony, rhythm, form, tempo, dynamics, and timbre. They develop knowledge of and use appropriate music vocabulary. By reading and

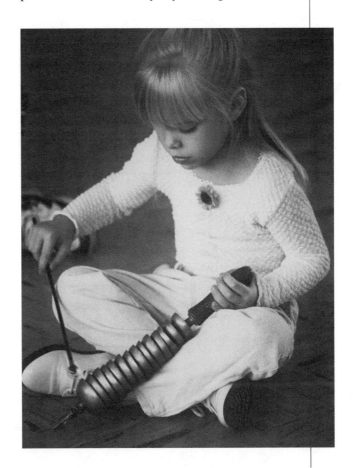

notating music, students learn written symbol systems for rhythm, pitch, dynamics, tempo, articulation, and expression.

Creative Expression

The creative expression of music occurs in the processes of performance, composition, and arrangement of music. The teacher's goal is to promote the joy of music and enable students to develop their musical skills so that they become capable and intelligent performers, creators, and audience members.

Musical understanding grows out of frequent experiences with music and sequential musical skill development. Singing is the most natural, intimate way for students actively to experience music. Students need to develop the skills to sing on pitch, in rhythm, and with expression. Group singing experiences include a wide repertoire of music from various styles and cultures.

Music, the most evanescent of the arts, never dies. . . . The Eroica Symphony *has a rebirth every time it is performed, and the* St. Matthew Passion *a resurrection whenever it is sung.*

—Angela Diller, *The Splendor of Music*

The playing of instruments from all parts of the world provides a powerful medium for learning music. Classroom music experiences with melodic, harmonic, and rhythmic instruments help young students develop musical concepts. Students develop the skills to perform on pitch, in rhythm, and with expression. Ensemble experiences include a wide repertoire of appropriate literature.

Choral ensembles and class instruction in wind, string, and percussion instruments through orchestra, band, and other ensemble classes should be available for those desiring to enhance their performing skills and musical intelligence.

Musical skills should include both performance of written music and participation in creative processes. Students also learn to improvise rhythms and melodies. They learn to harmonize parts consistent with the style, meter, and tonality of the music being studied. Students apply their musical understandings in composing and arranging music within specified guidelines in the creation of their own expressions.

Historical and Cultural Context

Every culture has characteristic, identifying music styles that help shape the cultural identity of each member of the culture. To a large degree the individual's artistic life is shaped by the surrounding culture. Music cannot be fully understood or appreciated without understanding the cultural context that gives life and meaning to the artistic expression.

It is essential to study music in the appropriate cultural context. But this direction in music education raises complex difficulties because it is much easier to teach a single musical style and not worry about the context than to teach the music of many cultures, the functions of music in those cultures, and the cultural and artistic values represented in the music. Colleges and universities need to provide prospective teachers with the necessary knowledge and skills to accomplish such tasks. Locating and using teaching resources for music from many cultures provides opportunities for students to enjoy the music of the whole world, to raise their cultural awareness, and to learn to live together in a humane and peaceful society.

Aesthetic Valuing

Aesthetic sensitivity extends beyond the acquisition of knowledge and skills to an understanding of the wide range of values in the arts. Aesthetic valuing of music involves comprehending the power and expression that music embodies. It is an outcome of meaningful activities in music in which students learn to think about and reflect on their responses to and engagement in music and to feel deeply about the music. Aesthetic valuing begins with artistic perception and extends to critical judgments about music. Teachers should provide frequent and varied musical experiences to which students can refer when making judgments about music.

Curriculum and Instruction in Music Education

All students need access to instruction in classroom or general music as well as to participation in choral and instrumental ensembles, and the instruction needs to be provided by credentialed music specialists. Classroom teachers reinforce music instruction by connecting music to the other arts and to other subject areas. The music curriculum at all levels needs to be student centered. Students from kindergarten through grade twelve need access to music classes that meet regularly during the school day to ensure the attainment of a comprehensive and sequential curriculum and continuity of learning.

Elementary School

All students in California elementary schools need to be engaged in appropriate music instruction in their regular classrooms. General music in the elementary school typically includes singing, rhythmic speech, movement, and the playing of pitched and nonpitched percussion instruments, recorders, and autoharps—all a part of the regular classroom experience at the elementary level. Students also need to be given the opportunity to explore their musical intelligence through participation in specialized performance groups. Choral and instrumental ensembles should be offered as electives during the school day. Instrument instruction

is developmentally appropriate as early as third or fourth grade.

Students in elementary schools need to be able to identify a variety of music from many cultures. They are introduced to and practice using the language of music in their discussions of composers and musical performances. Instruction helps students understand the historical and cultural contexts of music, styles, and periods and cultural group expressions. In addition, students in the elementary school need to have opportunities to identify and discuss the characteristics of master performances and compositions. This process enables students to learn about their own responses to music and to assess those responses in light of the music itself.

The elementary school music program provides opportunities for young students to explore a variety of music experiences—singing, playing an instrument, listening, responding—through instruction in the four

Music and Math Keep the Beat

Early elementary students begin their day by forming a large circle and singing a short song about math being fun and it's time to count. The teacher selects one student to stand in the center of the circle of students. This student is handed a beanbag. A couple of students are selected to play rhythm instruments. The student in the center begins the skip-counting game by announcing the counting system to be used (counting by twos or threes or fours and so on, starting at a particular number). Staying with the beat of the rhythm instruments, the student in the center begins by tossing the beanbag to one of the students in the circle. As that student catches the beanbag, he or she shouts out the first number in the series. For example, if students are counting by threes, the student answers "Three" and then tosses the beanbag back to the student in the center. That student then tosses the bag to another student, who must answer "Six"; and so on. If a student does not know the answer, or if his or her answer is not given in time with the beat, then that student moves to the center of the circle; and the game begins again. This activity improves concentration skills, teaches or reinforces basic mathematical facts, develops eye-hand coordination, and reinforces the musical concept of beat.

components and through varied instructional resources, including films, audio- and videotapes, photographs, instruments, and literature on music, that are appropriate for elementary school students. The exploration of a variety of music experiences promotes the students' personal and cultural understandings and insights and develops students' music knowledge and skills.

Middle School

The middle school music program continues to offer general music experiences for all students but also offers elective performing classes in orchestra, band, choir, and other ensembles. A well-developed program provides for beginning, intermediate, and advanced levels of student participation.

Instruction in the middle school develops a heightened perceptual awareness of the aesthetic qualities of the music of cultures throughout the world and of major works of music. Students develop listening skills, acquire knowledge of the natural and human-made environment, and become more perceptive and observant. Middle school music programs provide opportunities for students to apply the elements of music and extend their knowledge of and ability to use the language of music in verbal and nonverbal ways.

Students explore the creative process through their own music compositions and expressions. They study music compositions from many cultures and time periods in the cultural and historical context of their creation. Students develop the skills for making aesthetic judgments and engaging in thoughtful reasoning for those judgments.

High School

The high school music program should be an integral part of the school's visual and performing arts department. A high school music curriculum provides opportunities for students to begin in-depth studies in one or more areas of concentration.

Music instruction in the high school provides all students access to participation in choral and instrumental ensembles. These classes offer instruction at beginning, intermediate, and advanced levels to meet the needs of all students. Students also benefit from such classes as music appreciation, music theory, music history and literature, music keyboards and synthesizers, guitar, and the recording arts. Creative thinking in the four components of music education should be promoted

through a sequence of appropriate music courses. Connections of music to other curriculum areas expand and enrich the scope of the students' educational experience.

Students with Special Needs

The significance of the musical experience for students with special needs is not the degree of technical expertise that they achieve but the success they enjoy in reaching their greatest potential. Adaptations and modifications in instruction may be necessary, depending on the students' language, physical, and educational needs. For example, music and lyrics can be transcribed into Braille for students who are blind, and tapes can be prepared for study. The conductor's cues can be transmitted aurally by the breathing or touch of a partner musician in accordance with the conductor's preparatory motions.

Music programs in the elementary, middle, and high schools can provide students at risk of dropping out with the needed incentive to stay in school. These students may find a sense of connection and community in the music class, where each student's performance within a group tends to enhance the feeling of shared experience.

Students with limited English proficiency or those who speak English as a second language can also benefit greatly from a music program. These students can be integrated readily into music classes because communication occurs through instrumental or vocal demonstration of concepts and repetition of activities. For example, the learning of language in choral literature provides much-needed practice in a congenial and meaningful setting.

Students with obvious natural talent as musicians and performers require support and encouragement to enhance their gifts. At the same time teachers need to provide these

students with a balanced program and allow them to grow in skill or knowledge areas that do not come as easily to them.

Student Performances

Student performances provide opportunities for young musicians to demonstrate musical growth, gain personal satisfaction from achievement, and experience the joy of music making. Performances can motivate students to learn and can stimulate careful rehearsing. They are important experiences for student learning in music. However, performance should be an outcome rather than the basic objective of music instruction. An important objective of instruction is the advancement of each student's musical intelligence and understanding.

An active music program promotes music festivals for student musicians, composers, and performers; noontime concerts; festivals focusing on the works of a specific era; and collaborations with dance and theatre programs. Presentations of "performance in process" for peers and "performance to share" with the community should be included periodically, at the teacher's discretion, to meet the educational and artistic needs of the students.

Education of the student audience, as well as of the student musicians and performers, is an important consideration in the selection and performance of music. Program notes are helpful in audience education. Diversity must be a consideration in all aspects of music performance, including diversity in the selection of music to be performed, selection of solo performers, and preparation of the audience.

There is in all art a fine balance between the benefits of freedom and the benefits of confinement.

—Oscar Hammerstein II (1895–1960)

The visibility and popularity of student performing groups can result in performance expectations not directly related to music education. Demands are often made on school music ensembles to perform at athletic events, assemblies, student productions, parent meetings, community club meetings, conferences, and civic events. Although providing entertainment may be a valid activity of performance groups, it should never interfere with the students' music education.

Assessment in Music Education

Assessment in music focuses students' and teachers' attention on the inseparability of assessment and instruction. As indicated in Chapter 2, assessment becomes instruction when students and teachers reflect together on content standards or expectations of achievement and discuss ways of achieving those standards.

Wolf and Pistone enumerate five assumptions about the efficacy of assessment in the arts. First, both students and teachers insist on excellence of learning, as exhibited in performance. High standards are set, and

rehearsals and discussion involve ways in which to reach those standards. Second, there is much talk about judgment—opinions on a range of qualitative issues—and decisions based on insight, reason, and craft. Third, self-assessment is important for all artists and performers. Students need to learn how to understand and appraise their own work as well as that of their peers and other musicians and composers. Fourth, varied forms of assessment need to be utilized to obtain information about both individual and group performances. These forms are discussed in Chapter 2 and include everyday conversation and comments, critiques, and reviews. Fifth, continual assessment allows students to reflect on their own performance and use the insights gained from this process to enrich their work. Viewed in this way, assessment is an episode of learning.[3]

Wolf and her colleagues, who developed the handbook titled *Arts Propel: A Handbook for Music,* make an assumption that "ongoing assessment, both formal and informal, by students themselves and by teachers (in effect a dialogue about work and ways of working), yields revealing profiles of development and promotes learning and new levels of achievement."[4] For example, a project in music which connects creation, perception, and reflection in a particular student creation engages students in developing drafts of a composition, trying out notation systems, making tapes of practice sessions, and making suggestions about how to rehearse a work. In this activity the discipline necessary to produce music is reinforced, and the process of creating music is assessed at regular intervals—a process which becomes a part of good instructional practice.

The following example illustrates the way in which assessment directs student effort so

---

[3] D. P. Wolf and N. Pistone, *Taking Full Measure: Rethinking Assessment Through the Arts.* New York: College Entrance Examination Board, 1991.

[4] *Arts Propel: A Handbook for Music.* Edited by Ellen Winner. Cambridge, Mass.: Educational Testing Service and Harvard Project Zero, 1992.

that the result is satisfying to the teacher and student alike:

In a middle school music classroom, the teacher designed the following tasks that would culminate in the student's composition of a round. The production of a round summarizes learning that leads up to the culminating task. The production would join other examples collected for the student's portfolio.

1. Using their knowledge of and experience with the basic beat, placing beats in sets, using visual and auditory relationships of the tones within the major scale, and using a chord sequence, students design an original melody that is to be used as one voice in a three-voice round.

2. Students explain the social situations that led to the development and use of polyphonic texture in the music.

During the four weeks of the portfolio's development, students learned to sing descending scales accurately; filled in work sheets on scales and chords; learned "Alleluia," with understanding of the chord changes, cadences, and harmonic counterpoint; viewed movies about the Baroque era and about the life and works of J. S. Bach; learned to sing rounds; listened carefully and analytically to "For Unto Us a Child Is Born," from Handel's *Messiah*; designed their own melody for a round; and, finally, performed in groups of three.

During these activities essays were written, reflective journals compiled, audiotapes recorded and carefully analyzed, and discussions held between individual students and teachers about the students' progress.[5]

---

[5] This example of assessment in music is from Precious Bell Craft, a teacher at Will C. Wood Middle School in Sacramento, and is found in *Prelude to Performance Assessment in the Arts, Kindergarten Through Grade Twelve.* Sacramento: California Department of Education, 1993, pp. 23 and 28.

The Role of Technology in Music Education

Musicians have always been users of technology. Most musical instruments are products of centuries of technological development. In the early twentieth century, the recording of sound on records and tapes changed the way in which music was perceived and was taught. In the late twentieth century, the computer became a focal point for research, development, composition, and production.

The most powerful application for music education may be the use of computers in creating an environment for composition, improvisation, and arrangement of music. When connected to electronic instruments, computers can be used to record, transcribe, edit, and perform pieces of music. Such a musical environment enables experimentation and discovery learning. Use of the computer in transposition enables the teacher directly to accommodate the musical needs of students, such as providing the appropriate key for the rapidly changing voice. Computer-based instructional software for music includes tutorials and programs used for music theory and ear training, music games, and the testing of software.

Many other technological resources have direct applications for music instruction, including compact discs, CD-ROMs, video-discs, synthesizers, electronic keyboards, tone generators, drum machines, musical instrument digital interface (MIDI) connections, sequencers, sound samplers, and audio mixers.

The rapid change in technology will undoubtedly result in the emergence of new devices that will make this list incomplete. Music teachers must reflect on their instructional goals and determine how best to use the available resources for the most effective student learning. Budgets need to be designed to support technological development in music education. Technology is to be used not for its own sake but for the achievement of high-quality music education.

Every form of music is allied with some form of society and makes it easier to understand.

—Romain Rolland (1866–1944)

Teacher Preparation and Professional Development

The preservice education of a music educator provides for the development of a high degree of musicianship and an understanding of the processes of learning and the strategies of instruction appropriate to the ages and abilities of the students to be taught. The curricula of teacher education institutions need to be flexible and broad enough to accommodate the diversity of musical backgrounds, aptitudes, and needs of those preparing to teach music. Educating teachers for specialized areas in music education at institutions of higher education requires the provision of a flexible curriculum that includes preparation for the teaching of music for general education in the courses required for choral and instrumental majors.

The National Association of Schools of Music (NASM), the agency responsible for the accreditation of music curricula in higher education, recommends that music teacher education programs be composed of approximately 50 percent course work in music, 30 to 35 percent in general studies, and 15 to 20 percent in professional education (including student teaching). Music competencies that NASM considers essential for prospective music teachers include performing, analyzing, composing, arranging, and conducting music and possessing a varied repertory. Recommended teaching competencies include an understanding of child growth and development; an understanding of the philosophical and social foundations for music in education; the ability to assess aptitudes and interests of students and to devise appropriate learning experiences; knowledge of methods and materials for music education; the understanding and application of techniques for assessing the musical progress of students; and an awareness of the need for continual study and self-development to be a successful teacher.[6]

Classroom teachers who are expected to teach music in the primary grades need rigorous preservice training in music fundamentals and the process of developmentally appropriate music instruction. Such teachers often need to collaborate with music specialists who can regularly model effective music instruction, recommend resources, and provide support. The musical competence of the teacher of primary children is important if genuine musical learning is to occur.

Classroom teachers, as well as music specialists, need to know and understand how to use

---

[6] *NASM Handbook, 1989–1990.* Reston, Va.: National Association of Schools of Music, 1989.

the language of music, how to use resources that enhance students' knowledge of the context in which music is created and performed, and how to develop the students' capacity to think, speak, and write critically about music.

Professional development can occur through workshops, demonstrations, or exchanged classroom visits with peers; coaching or mentoring by district and county office specialists; courses at institutions of higher education; participation in meetings and conferences of state and national arts and educational professional organizations and agencies; and institutes and workshops, such as those offered by The California Arts Project (TCAP).

Professional development programs for classroom teachers can draw on the expertise of district music specialists, guest artists, and artists in residence. School districts are encouraged to support music coordinators and to provide for teachers' continual growth in music education. Classroom teachers should be encouraged to attend conferences and classes on methods for teaching general music in the elementary school and for integrating music with other subjects. Such opportunities are regularly offered by universities and professional organizations.

Resources, Environment, Materials, and Equipment

Educators can take advantage of the musical and cultural resources in their communities by collaborating with parents, churches, and civic organizations. Visits by local musicians, professional and amateur, enhance and bring into focus concepts already introduced in the regular instructional program. The music faculty and students at colleges and universities can provide a wealth of musical resources.

A well-planned music curriculum communicates an open invitation to community musicians to assist in promoting a lifelong love of music among students. Music educators can survey their communities for musicians willing to work and perform with students. In turn, music students can be encouraged to attend or participate in musical performances in the community. The inclusion of community resources strengthens the sequential, comprehensive music curriculum but cannot substitute for it.

The school district needs to provide current resources and equipment for the music curriculum. Sufficient up-to-date instructional resources are vital to school music programs. Music instruction requires an adequate budget for the purchase, maintenance, repair, and replacement of equipment and instruments. Musical instruments should be of high quality and in good condition. Sound equipment, such as compact-disc players, amplifiers, and speakers, must be of the highest quality and must be kept in good repair.

Goals for Music Education

Artistic Perception Component

Goal 1. *Students listen to and analyze music critically, using the vocabulary and language of music.*

Goal 2. *Students read and notate music.*

Creative Expression Component

Goal 3. *Students sing or perform on instruments a varied repertoire of music.*

Goal 4. *Students improvise melodies, variations, and accompaniments.*

Goal 5. *Students compose and arrange music.*

Historical and Cultural Context Component

Goal 6. *Students develop knowledge and skills necessary to understand and perform music from all parts of the world.*

Goal 7. *Students develop knowledge and understanding of the relationship of music to history and culture.*

Aesthetic Valuing Component

Goal 8. *Students apply knowledge, skill, and understanding to make critical judgments about and determine the quality of music experiences and performances.*

Goal 1. *Students listen to and analyze music critically, using the vocabulary and language of music.*

Examples of Knowledge and Skills for Goal 1

Kindergarten Through Grade Four	Grades Five Through Eight	Grades Nine Through Twelve Proficient	Grades Nine Through Twelve Advanced
Students identify simple forms and elements of music, when presented aurally.	Students describe specific music events in a given aural example, using appropriate terminology.	Students analyze an aural example of a varied repertoire of music representing diverse genres and cultures by describing the uses of elements of music and expressive devices.	Student musicians demonstrate their ability to perceive and remember music events by describing in detail significant events occurring in a given aural example.
Students demonstrate perceptual skills by moving to music, answering questions about music, and describing aural examples of music.	Students analyze the uses of elements of music (melody, harmony, rhythm, texture, form, dynamics, timbre) in given aural examples.	Students develop a technical vocabulary of music through essays and dialogue about the uses of elements of music in master compositions and contemporary works.	Student musicians compare the ways in which musical materials are used in a given example with the ways in which they are used in other works of the same genre or style.

Goal 2 *Students read and notate music.*

Examples of Knowledge and Skills for Goal 2

Students use a system to read simple rhythms, patterns, and pitch notations in the treble clef in major.	Students read at sight simple melodies in both the treble and bass clefs.	Students sight-read music accurately and expressively.	Student musicians sight-read music accurately and expressively, explaining pitch variations in both the bass and treble clefs.
Students identify symbols and traditional terms referring to dynamics, tempo, and articulation and interpret them correctly when performing.	Students identify and define standard notation symbols for pitch, rhythm, dynamics, tempo, articulation, and expression.	Students read an instrumental or vocal score of up to four staves and describe how the elements of music and the standard notation symbols are used.	Student musicians demonstrate their ability to read an instrumental or vocal score by describing the use of the elements of music and standard notational symbols and by explaining all transpositions and clefs.

Goal 3. *Students sing or perform on instruments a varied repertoire of music.*

Examples of Knowledge and Skills for Goal 3

Kindergarten Through Grade Four	Grades Five Through Eight	Grades Nine Through Twelve Proficient	Grades Nine Through Twelve Advanced
Students sing or perform on an instrument on pitch and in rhythm, with appropriate timbre, diction, and posture, and maintain a steady tempo.	Alone or in small and large ensembles, students sing accurately and with good breath control throughout the singing ranges or perform on at least one instrument accurately and independently, with good posture, playing position, and breath, bow, or stick control.	Students sing or perform on an instrument, with expression and technical accuracy, a varied repertoire of vocal or instrumental literature, including songs performed from memory.	Student musicians sing or perform on an instrument, with expression and technical accuracy, a large and varied repertoire of vocal or instrumental literature, Western and non-Western, including songs performed from memory.
Students sing ostinatos, partner songs, and rounds; or play an instrument, using short rhythms and melodic patterns.	Students sing music written in two and three parts or play simple melodies by ear on a melodic instrument and simple accompaniments on a harmonic instrument.	Students demonstrate well-developed ensemble skills and perform in small ensembles.	Student musicians sing or perform on an instrument in small ensembles or solo, demonstrating a knowledge of a varied repertoire, expression, and technical accuracy.

Goal 4. *Students improvise melodies, variations, and accompaniments.*

Examples of Knowledge and Skills for Goal 4

Students improvise "answers" in the same style to given rhythmic and melodic phrases.	Students improvise simple harmonic accompaniments.	Students improvise stylistically appropriate harmonizing parts to given rhythmic and melodic phrases.	Student musicians improvise stylistically appropriate harmonizing parts in a variety of styles—tonal and atonal.
Students improvise simple rhythmic and melodic ostinato accompaniments.	Students improvise melodic embellishments and simple rhythmic and melodic variations to given rhythmic and melodic phrases.	Students improvise rhythmic and melodic variations on given melodies.	Student musicians improvise original melodies in a variety of styles, over chord progressions, in a consistent style, meter, and tonality.

Goal 5. *Students sing or perform on instruments a varied repertoire of music.*

Examples of Knowledge and Skills for Goal 5

Kindergarten Through Grade Four	Grades Five Through Eight	Grades Nine Through Twelve Proficient	Grades Nine Through Twelve Advanced
Students create and arrange music to accompany readings or dramatizations.	Students compose short pieces within specified guidelines, demonstrating how the elements of music are used to achieve unity and variety, tension and release, and balance.	Students compose music in several distinct styles, demonstrating creativity in using the elements of music for expressive effect.	Student composers create music, demonstrating imagination and technical skill in applying the principles of composition.
Students use a variety of sound sources in composing simple melodies.	Students use a variety of traditional and nontraditional sound sources and electronic media in composing and arranging moderately complex melodies.	Students compose and arrange music for voices and various acoustic and electronic instruments, demonstrating knowledge of the ranges and traditional uses of the sound sources.	Student composers use music from other cultures as the influence on original compositions.

Historical and Cultural Context Component

Goal 6. *Students develop knowledge and skills necessary to understand and perform music from all parts of the world.*

Examples of Knowledge and Skills for Goal 6

Students listen to and describe aural examples of music of various styles representing diverse cultures.	Students analyze the uses of elements of music in aural examples representing diverse genres and cultures.	Students analyze aural examples of a varied repertoire of music, representing diverse genres and cultures, and describe the uses of the elements of music, including expressive devices.	Student musicians experience and analyze forms of microtonal music from other cultures.
Students identify a variety of instruments from various cultures and describe how they sound.	Students describe social functions of various musical forms.	Students identify cultural differences in describing and evaluating traditional music.	Student musicians analyze a variety of musical forms based on cultural styles, both tonal and microtonal.

Goal 7. *Students develop knowledge and understanding of the relationship of music to history and culture.*

Examples of Knowledge and Skills for Goal 7

Kindergarten Through Grade Four	Grades Five Through Eight	Grades Nine Through Twelve Proficient	Grades Nine Through Twelve Advanced
Students sing and dance from memory a varied repertoire of songs representing genres and styles from diverse cultures.	Students sing, dance, and perform music representing diverse genres and cultures, with expression appropriate for the work being performed.	Students sing or play with expression and technical accuracy a varied repertoire of vocal or instrumental literature from diverse cultures.	Student musicians perform with expression and technical accuracy a large repertoire of music from diverse cultures.
Students perform expressively a varied repertoire of music representing genres and styles from diverse cultures.	Students perform music from different cultures, demonstrating the uses and variations of the elements of music.	Students perform with expression and technical accuracy a varied repertoire of vocal or instrumental literature from diverse cultures.	Student musicians perform a variety of musical forms based on cultural styles, both tonal and microtonal.

Aesthetic Valuing Component

Goal 8. *Students apply knowledge, skills, and understandings to make critical judgments about and determine the quality of music experiences and performances.*

Examples of Knowledge and Skills for Goal 8

Students devise criteria for evaluating performances and compositions and apply the criteria in personal choices in music activities.	Students develop criteria for evaluating the quality and effectiveness of music performances and compositions and apply the criteria in their personal choices in listening and performing.	Students evaluate a performance, composition, or arrangement by comparing it to exemplary models, using criteria developed prior to the experience.	Student musicians evaluate a given musical work for its aesthetic qualities and explain the musical means it uses to evoke feelings and emotions.
Students explain and demonstrate, using appropriate music terminology, their personal preferences for specific musical works and styles.	Students evaluate the quality and effectiveness of their own and others' performances and compositions by applying specific criteria, appropriate for the style of the music, and offering constructive suggestions for improvement.	Students evolve specific criteria for making informed, critical judgments about the quality and effectiveness of performances, compositions, arrangements, and improvisations.	Student musicians compare formal classical criteria for evaluation with criteria developed for the evaluation of musical works from a variety of cultures.

Glossary: The Language of Music

atonality. The absence of tonality or of a tonal center.

baroque music. A style of European music developed between about 1600 and 1750. This exuberant and emotional style of music was explored in opera by Claudio Monteverdi and in the concerto by Johann Sebastian Bach and Antonio Vivaldi.

chord. The simultaneous combination of at least three different pitches.

classical music. A style of art music of any culture, as distinguished from folk or popular music or jazz; European music of the classical period, composed from about 1750 to 1825. Works by Franz Joseph Haydn, Wolfgang Amadeus Mozart, and Ludwig van Beethoven exemplify this style.

contemporary. Music or art that is current. In addition, artists, musicians, or composers who lived during the same historical periods as each other are known as contemporaries.

dynamics. The volume of sound; the loudness or softness of a musical passage.

elements of music. The sensory components used to create and talk about works of music. These components are *dynamics, form, harmony, pitch, rhythm, tempo, texture,* and *timbre* (see individual entries listed in alphabetical order).

expression. A quality that accounts for the specific emotional effect of music.

folk music. Traditional music that has evolved through the process of aural transmission. Well-known American practitioners of this style of music are Woody Guthrie and Jean Ritchie. Alan Lomax began recording the folk music of the Appalachian region during the 1930s.

form. The design of music, incorporating repetition, contrast, unity, and variety.

harmonic progressions. A succession of individual chords or harmonies which form larger units of phrases, sections, or compositions.

harmony. The vertical blocks of different tones that sound simultaneously; a progression of chords.

improvisation. Spontaneous musical invention.

interval. The distance in pitch between two tones.

jazz. A style of American music that originated in the South, started by African Americans; it is characterized by a strong, prominent meter; improvisation; and dotted or syncopated patterns. Early practitioners were Scott Joplin and W. C. Handy. Ma Rainey, Buddy Bolden, and Louis Armstrong, then Duke Ellington and Billie Holiday, brought the style to more popular status.

melody. A logical succession of musical pitches arranged in a rhythmic pattern.

meter. The pattern in which a steady succession of rhythmic pulses is organized.

microtonal. Intervals smaller than a semitone; a feature of Asian music.

MIDI. Musical instrument digital interface; a standardized "language" of digital bits that the computer can store.

ostinato. A rhythmic or melodic passage that is repeated continuously.

phrase. A musical idea, comparable to a sentence or a clause in language, which may be complete or incomplete.

pitch. The highness or lowness of sound, determined by the frequency of vibration.

rhythm. The combinations of long and short, even and uneven sounds that convey a sense of movement.

round. A composition in which the same melody is started at different times and sounded together; also called a canon.

score. Notation showing all the parts of a musical ensemble, aligned vertically on staves one above the other.

staff; stave. A series of five horizontal lines on which musical notes are written to indicate their pitch.

synthesizer. An electronic instrument used for the production of sound.

tempo. The pace at which music moves, based on the speed of the underlying beat.

texture. The character of the different layers of horizontal and vertical sounds.

timbre. The distinctive quality of tone of a sound.

tonality. A feeling in melody and harmony that one pitch, the tonic, is the pulling force or center of a piece of music.

tone. This term has multiple meanings: a sound of distinct pitch, quality, or duration; a musical note; the quality or character of a sound; an interval of a major second; a whole step; the characteristic quality or timbre of a particular instrument or voice.

Visual Arts Center Section

As Seen in a Work of Art

The color section of this framework provides a selection of reproductions of works of art that exemplify work by a particular artist, an art style, a technique or medium, or the art of varied cultures and periods. By studying works of art, students are inspired to research artists and their time period. They also gain an understanding of the significance of art history as they form a context for their own work and the current work of artists throughout the world. The impact of art on culture—from the earliest cave paintings to the most contemporary work and in societies throughout the world—is made evident through viewing, discussing, and researching important works in the visual arts.

In addition to their essential role in the visual arts curriculum, works of art provide students in history–social science and other subject areas with insights into a period of time and the values of a culture. In a visual way works of art relate beliefs, issues, experiences, and points of view.

The works presented in this color section correlate with key ideas in the *History– Social Science Framework* at various grade levels. In the citation for each work, the grade level and the key ideas are mentioned as well as ideas for connections to visual arts instruction. Many of the works pictured are mentioned in the framework; for example, the Bayeux Tapestry and the Vietnam War Memorial.

Study prints, slides, color transparencies, videos, CD-ROMs, and videodisks all provide rich resources of works by recognized artists from the past and present. *Course Models for the History–Social Science Framework,* published by the California Department of Education, lists additional resources. Many visual arts textbooks provide resources with their programs, and local museums, galleries, and arts providers may provide a rich source of visual materials for the classroom.

The works of art presented in this center section are but a few examples of the many pieces that might be used in a core or integrated approach to teaching the visual arts. District curriculum specialists and teachers are encouraged to develop similar examples for the visual arts as well as for the other arts disciplines and core subjects.

The California Department of Education gratefully acknowledges the individuals and organizations noted in the credit line for each work of art for the use of the reproductions that appear in this center section.

Frida Kahlo. *Frida and Diego Rivera.* **1931; oil on canvas, 39 3/8 x 31 in.** San Francisco Museum of Modern Art. Albert M. Bender Collection. Gift of Albert M. Bender.

Grade Two: Students talk about "People Who Make a Difference," including people from many cultures, now and long ago. This work reflects Frida Kahlo's style and her mastery of the self-portrait as she depicts herself in classic Mexican dress hand in hand with her husband. Second-grade students may do self-portrait drawings or collages.

Diego Rivera. *Detroit Industry, North Wall Cartoon—Vaccine.* **1932-33; mural.** Photograph © The Detroit Institute of Arts, 1995. Gift of Edsel B. Ford.

Grade Eleven: Focuses on the twentieth century, when Diego Rivera painted fresco murals in Mexico and the United States in the Mexican mural tradition. His works reflect his culture and his social and political beliefs. In this work he created a tribute to Detroit and the worker by depicting every step in the job of manufacturing the 1932 Ford V-8 automobile.

Ansel Adams. *Moon and Half Dome, Yosemite National Park, California.* © 1995 by the Trustees of the Ansel Adams Publishing Rights Trust. All rights reserved.

Grade Four: Includes study of "California: A Changing State." *Grade Nine:* Includes study of "Our State in the Twentieth Century" and "Physical Geography." Students may develop questions regarding the environment by reflecting on this photograph of Half Dome. They learn about photographic experimentation and photography as an art form from the work of Ansel Adams. They may discuss framing, vantage point, light and shadow, and balance. In this work light is used to define the natural forms, create contrast, pick out textures and details, and structure the photograph.

Lynn Hershman. *Camera Woman.*

Grade Twelve: Discusses contemporary issues, including technology and, perhaps, a survey of electronic arts. This work is a gelatin silver print from the series Phantom Limb (30" x 40", edition of 8, 1990). The artist has combined human parts and machine parts to underline our reliance on technology and media and the effects of the media on our identity and our picture of ourselves.

The Parthenon. Acropolis, Athens, Greece. Alinari/Art Resource, New York.

Grade Six: Includes study of the ancient Greeks and the early democratic forms of government. This picture of the Parthenon leads to reflection on the enduring cultural contributions of Greek architecture, ancient influences on contemporary style, and public art. Students may do projects and research on architecture and the use of perspective.

Maya Lin. *Vietnam War Memorial.* Smithsonian Institution Photo No. 90-11498.

Grade Twelve: Includes study of comparative governments as well as contemporary issues. The need for this memorial and the memorial itself have stimulated many political and aesthetic discussions. Students reflect on the emotional and political impact of public art, the healing power of the arts, and large-scale, site-specific sculpture.

Frederic-Auguste Bartholdi. *The Statue of Liberty.*

Grade Eight: Includes study of "The Rise of Industrial America." The Statue of Liberty promotes reflection on the relationships among nations, a statue as a symbol for America, casting and assemblage techniques used in sculpture, political art, and art in public places. The effects of the environment on works installed outside and proportions of the human figure used in large-scale sculpture are also topics for discussion and research.

Kano Tan'yu. *Confucius at the Apricot Altar and His Two Disciples.* **17th century, Japan, Edo Period, 1602–97; one of three panels, each 104.2 x 74.8 cm.** Courtesy Museum of Fine Arts, Boston. Fenollosa-Weld Collection.

Grade Six: Includes study of Confucian society and the flourishing of art, literature, and learning during this period. Students discuss the varying roles of artists and art in different cultures at different times and may learn Chinese brush painting techniques. Also appropriate for the Grade 2 "Developing Awareness of Cultural Diversity: Now and Long Ago" unit.

Walt Disney. *Mickey Mouse,* © 1966 Walt Disney Productions, World Rights Reserved. From the Givens collection.

Grade Eleven: Includes study of "The Great Depression" and "American Society in the Postwar Era." Mickey Mouse depicts how a nation deals with change. Art students concentrate on the history of cartoon art and animation and the influence of computers on the visual arts.

Michelangelo Buonarroti. *Moses,* **from the tomb of Pope Julius II. S. Pietro in Vincoli, Rome, Italy.** Scala/Art Resource, New York.

Grade Seven: Includes study of Europe during the Renaissance. Appropriate topics for discussion are the role of art in religion; the power of art to communicate ideas; the Renaissance master artist and the apprentice system; and the interest in all the arts at this moment in history, including works in literature by such writers as Shakespeare, Cervantes, and Machiavelli. Other topics might include the effects of advances in technology on the artist, the human figure in art, marble sculpture, and proportion in sculpture.

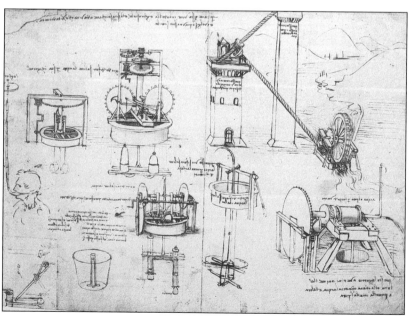

Leonardo da Vinci. *Folio 386 from Codex Atlanticus,* **with drawings of machinery.** Biblioteca Ambrosiana, Milan, Italy. Art Resource, New York.

Grade Seven: Focuses on the Renaissance and the effects of that period on present-day culture as well as the life of a Renaissance artist, including that of Leonardo da Vinci. He was involved in multiple areas of study and used drawing as a process of discovery, invention, and visualization.

Claude Monet. *Water Lily Pool.* **1900; oil on canvas, 89.9 x 101 cm.** Lewis Larned Coburn Memorial Collection. Photograph © 1994, The Art Institute of Chicago. All rights reserved.

Grade Ten: Includes study of "Unresolved Problems of the Modern World" when the Impressionists in France were responding to light in their new and unique way. Students do projects that focus on surface illusion rather than structural form and may discover the effect that outdoor lighting has on the way an artist sees color. The emotional potential of colors and brush strokes may also be explored.

Thornton Dial, Sr. *Top of the Line.* **1993; enamel, rope, metal on plywood, 60 $^3/_4$ x 81 x 5 $^1/_2$ in.** National Museum of American Art, Smithsonian Institution. Gift from the collection of Ron and June Shelp.

Grade Twelve: Includes study of "Contemporary Issues in the World Today" and socioeconomic equality in contemporary America. Done in mixed media by black American artist Thornton Dial, this work is his comment on the 1992 Los Angeles riots. It stimulates discussion of contemporary socioeconomic issues.

Prince Riding an Elephant

Grade Six: Includes study of early civilization of India. This leaf from an album illustrates emphasis, in the work of this time and culture, on decorative effects rather than on modeling that considers conventional light sources. Students may observe the flat and ornamental qualities and discuss pictorial invention, imagination, and formal considerations. This item is also appropriate for grades one and two when other cultures are being studied.

Bayeux Tapestry: Battle Between English and Normans. 11th century. Musee de la Tapisserie, Bayeux, France. Giraudon/Art Resource, New York.

Grade Six: Includes study of the Norman invasion of England and the Norman victory at Hastings in A.D. 1066, which is the topic depicted in the Bayeux Tapestry. Visual art topics include the status of women artists in the Middle Ages; fiber art, such as embroidery; tapestry and weaving techniques; and the depiction of an epic story episode by episode.

Two Bison. **Altamira Caves, Spain.**
Scala/Art Resources, New York

Grade Six: Includes study of early
humankind and the development of human
societies. Students observe the use of line
and discuss the materials used for the cave
paintings. They also reflect on the purpose
and function of art, the beginning of art
history, the conceptual step taken by human
beings from depicting form in three
dimensions to two dimensional
representation, and the use of a
monochromatic color scheme.

George Caleb Bingham. ***Daniel Boone Escorting Settlers Through the Cumberland Gap.*** **1851-52;
oil on canvas, 149 x 255 in.** Washington University Gallery of Art, St. Louis, Missouri. Gift of Nathaniel
Phillips, Boston, 1890.

Grade Five: Includes study of the settling of the Trans-Appalachian West. In this painting Bingham
realistically depicts a historical event, giving it his own interpretation in a formal composition based on
the pyramid, using light and shadow to create a mood and atmosphere. Students enjoy reading biographies
of Daniel Boone and stories about the pathfinders.

Amida Nyorai. *Japanese Sculpture of Buddha.* **Wood with traces of lacquer, gilding, and pigment. Late Heian period, 12th century.** Asian Art Museum of San Francisco. The Avery Brundage Collection.

Grade Nine: Elective course in comparative world religions includes study of Buddhism. Students learn about Buddhist beliefs from a study of Eastern art. Includes a discussion of the use of religious figures as the subjects for sculpture and the yoga-like pose and meditative expression intrinsic to the Eastern religion of Buddhism.

***Portrait of Pharaoh Tutankhamen*, in gold and precious stones, from the inner coffin of the tomb. Sculpture, 1342 BCE.** Egyptian Museum, Cairo, Egypt. Erich Lessing/Art Resource, New York.

Grade Six: Includes study of the beginnings of civilization in Ancient Egypt. Students may discuss the role of sculptural objects in religion and politics; symbolism in art; portraits; and monuments to important people.

Horn Blower. **Nigeria. The Metropolitan Museum of Art. The Michael C. Rockefeller Memorial Collection. Gift of Nelson A. Rockefeller, 1972.**

Grade Nine: Elective courses, such as area studies (cultures, anthropology) or ethnic studies, benefit from an investigation of the visual arts of the area under study. A study of the bronzes of Benin reveals a powerful kingdom during the fifteenth century possessing great wealth displayed in bronze and ivory works of art. Traditional symbols and costumes can be traced through these works, which continued to be created until the 1890s.

The Great Calendar Stone. National Museum of Anthropology, Mexico City, Mexico. Art Resource, New York.

Grade Seven: Focuses on the civilizations of the Americas, including the achievements of the Aztecs. Students reflect on art as a recorder of history, picture writing, the function and definition of art, engraving, and stone sculpture. Also appropriate for the Grade 2 "Developing Awareness of Cultural Diversity: Now and Long Ago" unit.

Woodgatherers. University of New Mexico, Albuqerque. Maxwell Museum of Anthropology.

Grade Five: Includes study of "The Land and People Before Columbus." This classic black-on-white pottery bowl stimulates discussion of the art of American Indians, adjustment of people to their natural environment, knowledge gained from archeology, ceramics as functional and decorative, the chemistry of clay and glazes, and symbols in art. The work depicts a man and a woman with a dog. The man (far left) is drawn smaller to show distance, illustrating an early attempt at lateral perspective.

Ando Hiroshige. *Rain Shower on Olashi.* **Color woodblock print, 35.2 x 23.2 cm.** © The Cleveland Museum of Art. Gift from J. H. Wade.

Grade One: Focuses on "A Child's Place in Time and Space" and includes awareness of cultural diversity now and long ago and the many ways in which people are alike as well as different. This famous Japanese woodcut print stimulates discussion of people, places, and common events and introduces printmaking techniques, the depiction of space in art, and the use of diagonals in a composition. Hiroshige depicts nature as grand and people as small. The print can also be used effectively in the seventh grade when Japan is studied.

J. Cameron. *The Life of a Fireman: The Metropolitan System.* **1866.** Published by Currier & Ives. Museum of the City of New York. The J. Clarence Davies Collection.

Grade Two: Includes study of "People Who Make a Difference," including ancestors from long ago and a comparison of past to present. The realistic lithographs of Currier & Ives show how artists record history and stimulate discussions of the past and important people in our community. This print depicts a fire company in New York City in 1866 with the first steam-propelled fire engine. Also appropriate for kindergarten, as part of "Learning and Working Now and Long Ago."

Charles Nahl. *Sunday Morning in the Mines.* **1872; oil on canvas, 72 x 108 in.** Crocker Art Museum, Sacramento, California. E. B. Crocker Collection.

Grade Four: Includes study of the Westward Movement and the California Gold Rush. This painting illustrates how an artist can depict a historical context, including the activities of the people, their structures, and the natural environment. When viewing this realistic oil painting, we can almost hear the songs of the gold miners.

Raymond Saunders. *Charlie Parker.* **1977; enamel, masking tape, newsprint, and ink on canvas, 96 1/8 x 82 3/8 in.** San Francisco Museum of Modern Art. Gift of Mrs. and Mrs. Robert Krasnow.

Grade Nine: Elective course in humanities includes many discussions of how the arts are interrelated and how they reflect culture. In this work Saunders memorializes the late jazz musician who was called "Bird" by his friends and fans. A combination of painting and collage (the photograph is of an unidentified man), the work was commissioned by Warner Brothers Studios as a commemorative record jacket cover for a Charlie Parker album series. Raymond Saunders said that this piece was created after "walking through neighborhoods" thinking about Bird.

Howard Chandler Christy. *The Signing of the Constitution of the United States.* National Graphic Center, Falls Church, Virginia.

Grade Twelve: Begins with study of the U.S. Constitution and the Bill of Rights. This work stimulates discussion of the time, place, and individuals involved as well as discussions of portraiture and the role of art in documenting history.

Emanuel Leutze. *Washington Crossing the Delaware.* **1851; oil on canvas, 255 x 149 in.** The Metropolitan Museum of Art. Gift of John Stewart Kennedy, 1897.

Grade Three: Includes study of "Continuity and Change in Our Nation's History." Students meet extraordinary and ordinary people from long ago in art, literature, biographies, folktales, and legends. In this work the artist re-creates an important moment in the history of our country. This work shows the tension between balance, stability, and calm in the figure of Washington contrasted with a threatening, stormy environment and the struggles of his men.

Honoré Daumier. *The Third Class Carriage.* **Oil on canvas, 35 1/2 x 25 3/4 in.** The Metropolitan Museum of Art. Bequest of Mrs. H. O. Havemeyer, 1929. The H. O. Havemeyer Collection.

Grade Ten: Includes study of the Industrial Revolution. Daumier's lithographs, drawings, and paintings commented on social and political issues that carry over to present times. This oil painting illustrated daily life, with humble people of all ages jammed together on the wooden benches in a train. It is symbolic of the anonymity and displacement that came with the Industrial Revolution.

Barbara Kruger. *Untitled (It's a Small World).* **1990; photo silkcreen on vinyl, 103 x 143 in.** The Museum of Contemporary Art, purchased with funds provided by the NEA and Douglas S. Cramer. Photo credit: Paula Goldman.

Grade Nine: Focuses on "Women in Our History," an elective course that may include contemporary issues related to the feminist movement. This artist presents her point of view through a satirical work that causes us to examine our own attitudes. Employing a wide range of technologies in her work, Kruger sparks discussions on contemporary media used in art, activist women artists, and art as both political comment and a force for social change.

Richard Diebenkorn. *Berkeley #57.* **1955; oil on canvas, 59 ¹/₂ x 59 ¹/₂ in.** San Francisco Museum of Modern Art. Bequest of Joseph M. Bransten in memory of Ellen Hart Bransten.

Grade Four: Focuses on study of "A Changing State," including modern California and a consideration of immigration, technology, and cities. Diebenkorn did many landscapes that reflect his interpretation of different parts of California. Students might discuss the qualities of city life and the reflection of those qualities in this abstract painting.

Wayne Thiebaud. *Sunset Streets.* **1985; oil on canvas, 48 x 35 ³/₄ in.** San Francisco Museum of Modern Art. Purchased with the aid of funds from public subscriptions, William L. Gerstle Fund, Fund of the 80's, Thomas and Shirley Davis, Clinton Walker Fund, and Thomas Weisel.

Grade One: Study of "A Child's Place in Time and Space" addresses children's growing sense of place and spatial relationships and makes possible new geographic learning. This work depicts the artist's view of a steep San Francisco street and may inspire students to draw pictures or create a mural of their neighborhood.

The clear expression of life, so phrased and disclosed that it awakens a profound sense of recognition or discovery in the audience-mind, is to me the greater purpose of the theatre. And, of course, it is the playwright who must first see and understand that rare essence of significant truth that goes to make a play.

—Gilmor Brown,
founder, Pasadena Playhouse

From the earliest known times, theatre has been explicitly reflective of its time. Religious and historical commemorations, celebration, and honor have all found their voices in the theatre. Through storytelling, other verbal traditions, and dramatizations, cultures have retained the legends and folklore that help educate their members. Today, many kinds of events in this culture are commemorated through pageant and theatre. Dramatization is a powerful way in which to reflect on the issues and challenges of society.

Theatre is a collaborative art that enhances communication and is accessible to all students, whether through acting, direction, script writing, media, design, or production. Students build their communication skills through storytelling, puppetry, pantomime, improvisation, and formal acting, assessing their progress on the way. Experience with each of these communication forms provides a complete theatrical experience.

Theatre also provides students with invaluable skills for comprehending and analyzing the barrage of visual and aural information that has become a part of modern life. Students construct meaning from their past experiences. Through engagement in theatre experiences, students understand how those who control the media use the elements and principles of theatre to enable viewers to construct meaning in specific ways. By participating in theatre, students learn the elements of presentation and the power of the media in influencing and manipulating information and opinion.

The many-faceted nature of theatre allows students to learn through multiple intelligences, as described by Gardner.[1] Theatre allows students to extend their capacity for learning through these varied forms of intelligence: linguistic intelligence, devel-

---

[1] Howard Gardner, *Frames of Mind: The Theory of Multiple Intelligences* (Tenth anniversary edition). New York: Basic Books, Inc., 1993.

oped through script writing, acting, storytelling, and improvisation; logical-mathematical intelligence, developed through technical theatre, multimedia production, and stage management; spatial intelligence, developed through direction and design; musical intelligence, developed through sound effects and musical accompaniments to productions; bodily-kinesthetic intelligence, developed through acting, direction, choreography, and pantomime; interpersonal intelligence, developed through ensembles and house and stage management; and intrapersonal intelligence, developed through imagery, characterization, script writing, and creative drama.

Every aspect of theatre, from the interpretation of a familiar folk tale in a kindergarten class through the editing of a video portfolio project in high school, is composed of numerous challenges that must be addressed and choices that must be made. Students involved in theatre are constantly thinking, experimenting, creating, reflecting, and revising—processes that will serve them throughout their lives.

Theatre is more influential today than ever before, reaching millions of people worldwide. Cutting-edge technology infuses theatre into people's lives. California is the world center of film and electronic media. Providing instruction in theatre arts helps students become responsible workers in those fields, informed consumers and citizens, effective communicators, and leaders who are not easily manipulated or influenced by the media.

Experimentation is at the heart of the learning process. Although finished pieces for the stage or screen are a part of a complete theatre program, teachers should not feel that producing a show is always the goal.

Students need to experience all forms of theatre in a carefully structured program of many cultures, including those related to the local community. A fully inclusive program should embrace both sexes, encourage all body types and sizes, respect ethnic diversity, and provide for students with special needs.

A theatre program needs to:

1. Be well planned and developmentally appropriate, from kindergarten through grade twelve.

2. Provide opportunities for guided reflection about and analysis of theatre performances in many forms, including film and video.

3. Provide opportunities for personal skill development, with emphasis on the creative process as well as the product.

4. Develop informed citizens with a lifelong commitment to the arts.

5. Develop students' appreciation for and understanding of the theatre of many cultures and periods in world history.

At this time California does not issue a theatre teaching credential. When one is available, credentialed theatre specialists and trained generalists will be able to offer a comprehensive theatre program. For now, the theatre specialist, artist in residence, or district theatre specialist needs to collaborate with the district curriculum specialist and the classroom teacher to design an effective theatre curriculum.

The Four Components of Theatre Education

Students growing up in an information-oriented world absorb much of their knowledge from electronic media. It is essential for students to be knowledgeable about the power and influence of the media so that they can think for themselves and make constructive criticisms and judgments about the kinds of programs and films being presented for their viewing and listening. When students produce, direct, and act in their own original productions, they understand another dimension of theatre as an art form. Effective theatre instruction incorporates the four components of arts education: artistic perception, creative expression, historical and cultural context, and aesthetic valuing.

Whenever and wherever humans have progressed beyond the mere struggle for physical existence, . . . there has been theatre in some sense: an inevitable place for acting, dancing, dialogue, drama in the ordered scheme of life.

—Sheldon Cheney (1886–1980)

Artistic Perception

Artistic perception in theatre is the process of observing the environment and constructing meaning from it. The process involves and develops the acuity of all the senses. Whether improvised or scripted, a production is the expression of the perceptions of the writer, the director, the actors, and the designers. Response by the audience requires perception based on knowledge of theatre technique.

Inherent in this component is the appreciation for imagination and creativity. Students learn the vocabulary of theatre through direct experiences with the terms and concepts. Engagement in theatre experiences enables students to heighten their sensitivity to their own and others' potential for creation. Through this heightened awareness and perception, students learn that otherwise ordinary experiences take on an artistic dimension.

Creative Expression

Creative expression is both process and product. The process of developing proficiency in acting, direction, use of the media, production, and script writing results in theatre products of creative expression that embody the students' perceptions. Students develop skills through exploration, reflection, revision, and self-reflection. All students can participate in and experience success because the nature of theatre inspires personal involvement and investment of energy, which often lead to a polished performance.

Direct personal involvement in these expressive modes is necessary for one to understand and appreciate theatre. Purposeful student theatre activities focus on, encourage, and provide a channel for communication and originality and enhance students' understanding of the structure and language of theatre. The artistic perception appropriate to theatre is embodied in the creative expression of performance.

Historical and Cultural Context

There are two basic aspects to exploring historical and cultural context in theatre. The first is the time and culture captured in theatrical works; the second is the history of cultures in theatre itself.

In theatre the conventions, mores, and standards of a culture come alive. Theatre allows students to look at the world through the lens of a particular place and time. Students gain appreciation of their own and other cultures and make connections between issues confronted in the past and problems to be solved today. They may also be introduced to other cultures through creative drama or theatre activities involving world dramatic literature, folklore, myths, storytelling, personal histories, and puppetry. Theatre surprises and inspires students as they discover the spectrum of theatrical forms across time and place.

Theatre itself is an important part of culture and history. Students gain a greater understanding of the art and a broader perspective from which to create their own works by knowing the history of dramatic literature, technology, architecture, acting styles, and theatre conventions that have developed into contemporary world theatre.

Aesthetic Valuing

Theatre is a universal language that speaks to the heart and mind. Aesthetic valuing extends the vocabulary with which one can express the feelings, thoughts, and ideas elicited by theatrical experiences. Informed judgments, an integral part of theatre based on opportunities for observation and practice across a broad range of experiences, depend on an understanding of the intent, structure, effectiveness, and worth of a play, movie, television drama, or other theatrical presentation. The valuing process is cyclical and cumulative; students reflect on, analyze, and evaluate their own work. This process gives them the experience and confidence to assess the work of others. Critiquing the work of others creates new vantage points for students from which they can review their own work.

Students in theatre have the opportunity to discover the difference between theatre reviews and dramatic criticism; acquire the ability to think and speak about aspects of theatre with reason and intelligence; and discuss multifaceted theatre experiences from a variety of viewpoints.

Curriculum and Instruction in Theatre Education

The theatre arts program needs to be designed to promote the development of each student's imagination, knowledge, problem-solving ability, understanding of human relationships, and communication skills. School administrators and the theatre arts specialist or theatre arts teacher need to establish a carefully planned program of theatre instruction for each elementary, middle, and high school student. When plays are performed, they should be chosen for their educational worth, literary merit, diversity, and cultural contribution.

Elementary School

All students in California elementary schools need to be engaged in appropriate classroom theatre experiences in their regular classrooms. Theatre in the elementary school typically includes creative dramatics, improvisation, pantomime, storytelling, and the acting out of stories, among many other forms. All students need to be given the opportunity to explore their creative potential through participation in specialized performance groups.

An elementary school theatre program provides developmentally appropriate, creative drama experiences for all students, including theatre games, improvisation, role playing, group experiences, and ensemble work. All children should have the opportunity to participate in creative drama activities for their intrinsic value and for their value as a process through which the students may learn about other subjects.

Schools should provide instruction and presentation materials, including films, audio- and videotapes, prints, photographs, props, and literature on theatre, that are appropriate for elementary school students. Exposing students to a variety of experiences in theatre provides them with the opportunities to define personal and cultural insights and historical understanding as well as develop knowledge and skills about theatre.

Middle School

A middle grades theatre program continues creative drama classes for all students and offers elective performance classes in beginning, intermediate, and advanced theatre. A well-developed program provides students with opportunities to continue developing their skills and their understanding of theatre and to perform in formal and informal productions.

Middle schools provide theatre instruction in exploratory, elective, and special-interest classes. Theatre instruction is also included during arts-infused interdisciplinary and thematic-based instruction in core curriculum classes, such as English–language arts and history. Theatre instruction in the middle grades is related to the developmental stages and interests of the young adolescent. Instruction includes experiences for individual students or collaborating groups of students. The young adolescent often assists in the definition of the artistic problem.

High School

The high school theatre program should be an integral part of the school's visual and performing arts department. A high school theatre curriculum provides opportunities for students to begin in-depth studies in one or more areas of concentration.

A theatre curriculum at the high school level includes courses in performance; design; and historical, cultural, and aesthetic valuation. Theatre teachers and school administrators need to work together to develop a vision of the school's program that encompasses the goals and expectations presented later in this chapter under "Goals for Theatre Education." Courses are offered in beginning, intermediate, and advanced theatre; play production; and stagecraft (including design and management). Larger schools provide a wide diversity of additional course offerings, including but not limited to electronic media, dramatic literature, and oral interpretation.

High school theatre teachers need to communicate in an ongoing manner with their colleagues in university theatre departments and professional theatre companies. This communication will enhance their programs

Page to Stage: An Interdisciplinary, Cross-Grade Theatre Project

An elementary school collaborates with a high school in the same district to write and perform plays. Throughout the year the classroom teachers collect writing assignments, such as short stories or biographies of historical men and women, from elementary school students in all grades and at all skill levels. The students' writings are read and discussed in intermediate and advanced acting classes at the high school, and a few are selected to be developed into short plays. Parents are notified of the writing selections and the performance of the plays. The high school acting students work as an ensemble to develop short plays based on the selected writings. Finally, the high school acting students perform the plays and, after the performance, discuss the work with the elementary school audience. The young playwrights and cast members receive certificates recognizing their participation in bringing the "page to the stage." This empowerment of the writing experience increases the students' self-esteem and establishes a community of student authors and actors.

and support the continuity of instruction. There are often community college or university theatre intern programs in design and direction that may be open to the high school theatre teacher or to students with particular interests or talents.

Students with Special Needs

All students can and should participate in a theatre program that provides a social context in which they can make meaning through exploration, interaction, risk taking, assessment, reflection, and refinement of their experiences.

In theatre students explore their limitations and their gifts. The multifaceted nature of theatre allows all students to find their own areas of interest and strength. The program needs to allow for maximum participation of every student in every aspect of the theatre experience. The teacher of theatre sensitively encourages students to push the boundaries of their abilities.

Students at risk of dropping out of school who may not show interest in other subject areas will often blossom in creative drama or theatre performance classes in which they can express themselves safely. Through the collaborative processes, with peer and teacher support, the theatre program provides a creative outlet and an opportunity for introspection so that students at risk of dropping out build self-esteem, make meaningful friendships, grow in self-discipline, develop problem-solving abilities, plan for the world of work and further education, strengthen their support systems, and make connections with other core subjects, thereby increasing their interest in school.

Access and accommodations should be provided for students with learning and physical disabilities. In the classroom the teacher selects exercises that allow all students to express their ideas. In production

situations the teacher thoughtfully considers the choice of the play, the design of the set, the venue, nontraditional casting, and alternative stage techniques, such as student partnering (e.g., one student interpreting the vocal aspects of a character and another the physical aspects) and technical support teams. Students who are deaf should be encouraged to use and develop sign language and other communication skills in classroom activities and production. Modern electronic technologies allow the most severely language-impaired students to participate in theatre through the use of augmentative communication devices.

Students can gain understanding of one another by using each other as resources in character development, especially when a characterization requires knowledge of a specific cultural, ethnic, or religious group. Such sensitivity assists in making productions more accessible to a wider range of audiences through the use of student sign language interpreters, descriptive narrators, and translators. Guest artists (working with students in the classroom as well as perform-

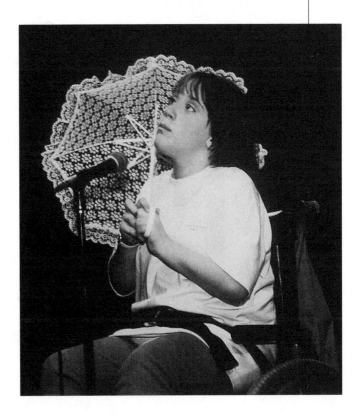

ing for them) who represent a variety of theatrical forms, cultures, languages, backgrounds, and physical challenges can provide positive role models for students.

Students with limited English proficiency are provided countless opportunities to demonstrate concepts nonverbally through movement, direction, media, and design and many opportunities to practice language in a supportive environment through improvisation, script writing, and the process of collaboration. Students who are new arrivals to the country have a safe environment in which to practice social, interactive skills with their classmates as they share aspects of their own backgrounds through creative drama.

Student Performances

Although not all theatre activities will or should culminate in student performances, they are an integral part of the theatre as art and should be included at all school levels, with appropriate modifications. Performance should be experienced in the full spectrum of theatre, including traditional production, improvisation, mime, film, and the electronic media. An active theatre arts program promotes one-act play festivals by student writers; "lunch-box" or noontime theatre; festivals centering on the works of major playwrights; dance-mime programs; multimedia festivals and performances; and fully produced plays that provide images of excellence in character, content, theme, values, and performance. Presentations of "performance in process" for peers and "performance to share" with the community should also be included periodically, at the teacher's discretion, to meet the educational and artistic needs of students.

Education of the student audience, as well as of the student performers, is an important consideration in the selection and production of plays. Performers need to know *who* their audience is, and the audience needs to be instructed how to respond appropriately to the performance. Program notes are helpful in audience education. Diversity must be a consideration in all aspects of theatre production, including the selection of cast and crew members and the selection of scripts.

Through theatre all students can experience the importance of their individual contributions outside the family. Both student-created plays and educationally valid formal plays should be offered as programs for student and parent audiences.

Student performance in nonprofessional theatre productions should be an extension of classroom training. The quality of performance must provide a positive aesthetic experience for the players and the audience. Any student in a theatre arts program who demonstrates a commitment to the art and accepts the discipline required of a performer should be given opportunities to perform at school or with community groups. The qualified teacher of theatre arts should have the final word in determining performance readiness.

Assessment in Theatre Education

Assessment in theatre focuses students' and teachers' attention on the inseparability of assessment and instruction. As indicated in Chapter 2, assessment becomes instruction when students and teachers reflect together on standards or expectations of achievement and discuss ways of achieving those standards.

Wolf and Pistone enumerate five assumptions about the efficacy of assessment in the arts. First, both students and teachers insist on excellence of learning, as exhibited in performance. High standards are set, and rehearsals and discussion involve ways in which to reach those standards. Second, there is much talk about judgment—opinions on a range of qualitative issues—and decisions based on insight, reason, and craft. Third, self-assessment is important for all artists and performers. Students need to learn how to understand and appraise their own work as well as that of their peers. Fourth, varied forms of assessment need to be utilized to

obtain information about both individual and group performances. These forms are discussed in Chapter 2 and include everyday conversation and comments, critiques, and reviews. Fifth, continual assessment allows students to reflect on their own performance and use the insights gained from this process to enrich their work. Viewed in this way, assessment is an episode of learning.[2]

Wolf and her colleagues, who developed the handbook titled *Arts Propel: A Handbook for Music,* make an assumption that "ongoing assessment, both formal and informal, by students themselves and by teachers (in effect a dialogue about work and ways of working), yields revealing profiles of development and promotes learning and new levels of achievement."[3]

The following example illustrates the way in which assessment directs student effort so

---

[2] D. P. Wolf and N. Pistone, *Taking Full Measure: Rethinking Assessment Through the Arts.* New York: College Entrance Examination Board, 1991.

[3] *Arts Propel: A Handbook for Music.* Edited by Ellen Winner. Cambridge, Mass.: Educational Testing Service and Harvard Project Zero, 1992.

that the result is satisfying to the teacher and student alike:

In an elementary school an assessment designed for kindergarten-through-grade-three students centered on an open-ended problem associated with the annual school play. Students were given free choices of the roles they wanted to act out, and their solutions to the problem were their performances.

The students were given careful instruction about movement, voice projection, and their positions while on stage. The students and teacher together developed a scoring rubric that reflected achievement goals. For a few weeks the students practiced their self-selected lines and movements. Videotapes were made of practices so that they could clearly see their own performances.

A videotape was also made of the final performance, presented before parents and friends. After this performance, when they were back in the classroom, the students and teacher applied the rubric for the self-evaluation. Discussion about movement and use of the voice resulted in general agreement that success meant "being in the role the whole time we were on stage." The class watched the videotape of the final performance and practiced using the self-evaluation scale. After looking at the videotape again, each student circled the number that applied to his or her performance.

The key to this assessment was the careful training the teacher gave the students about evaluating their own performance. The teacher helped them develop the criteria for judging themselves, then guided them in the use of the scale.[4]

---

[4] This example of assessment in theatre is adapted from one devised by Steven Mitchell, a teacher in the Trinity Center Elementary School District. It is found in *Prelude to Performance Assessment in the Arts, Kindergarten Through Grade Twelve*. Sacramento: California Department of Education, 1993, pp. 37–38.

The Role of Technology in Theatre Education

In theatre technology may be used as a product, a process, or a resource in instruction and for assessments. Video, film, and electronic media, which are now available to many schools, provide opportunities for education in the four components of artistic perception, creative expression, historical and cultural context, and aesthetic valuing. A complete theatre program needs to include the use of electronic media in viewing, producing, and evaluating productions and for the historical and cultural study of theatre.

Advances in stagecraft, such as computerized lighting controllers, sound-mixing equipment, design software, desktop publishing, and special effects, are now affordable and are available for use in schools. Multimedia products incorporating live theatre with electronic media are also options to be explored. CD-ROMs, laser discs, and the information highway provide burgeoning access to technical information, theatre productions, multimedia presentations, communication, scripts, journals, and media reviews that suggest ways in which to use theatre in the classroom.

Using technology for assessment is one of the most valuable applications for theatre teachers. Recording student rehearsals and performances on videotape permits students to evaluate and reflect on their work. Video portfolios can be economically duplicated, stored, and shared with others, developing in students a sense of history, progress, and accomplishment.

Teacher Preparation and Professional Development

Teachers are best prepared to teach theatre when they have majored in theatre in their college or university undergraduate program. In addition, the inclusion of theatre in the core of courses required of single-subject and multiple-subjects credential programs in colleges and universities helps prepare all teachers to teach the knowledge and skills of theatre. Prospective teachers need to understand the processes of learning and strategies of instruction appropriate to the ages and abilities of students. Teachers of theatre need to have the same academic preparation in their discipline as do teachers in other core disciplines.

School districts are encouraged to support theatre specialists and to provide for teachers' continual professional growth in theatre. Teachers need to be encouraged to enroll in theatre courses in local colleges and universities and be allowed opportunities to participate in special workshops offered by their professional organization in theatre.

Theatre teachers or generalists in kindergarten through grade six need to be able to provide an environment that fosters students' love of performance. This objective can be achieved principally when teachers know and teach the basic elements of theatre, including creative drama. In addition, teachers need to know how to lead students in expressing and experiencing theatre through structured improvisation and creative problem solving.

The theatre teacher at the middle and high school levels should be able to structure and teach specialized theatre technique classes appropriate to students' skill levels, needs, and interests. At those levels teachers also need to be able to recognize talented theatre students and challenge them, through referrals to other special learning environments and opportunities, to expand their talents.

Professional development can occur through workshops, demonstrations, or exchanged classroom visits with peers; coaching and mentoring by district and county office specialists; courses at institutions of higher education; participation in meetings and conferences of state and national arts and educational professional organizations and agencies; and institutes and workshops, such as those offered by The California Arts Project (TCAP).

Resources, Environment, Materials, and Equipment

Elementary school theatre programs need flexible classroom playing areas or a large, open playing space. They also need a storage

area in classrooms for props, costumes, and curriculum materials. Desirable equipment includes a compact-disc player, an audio player and recorder, a video camera, a videocassette recorder, a television monitor, laser discs, and computers for research, design, and word processing.

Middle school theatre programs need the same equipment for their theatre classrooms as do the elementary school programs. The middle school program also needs an assembly hall or other large room with a stage or platform equipped with lighting, sound equipment, and curtains and seating for an audience.

High school theatre programs need two learning environments: (1) a classroom and resource center; and (2) a theatre or auditorium. The resource center should contain varied materials, such as the following:

- Books (theatre texts, plays, scenes, monologues, history of theatre, historical references and biographies)

- Professional theatre and media journals and magazines

- Electronic media library, with videos of master plays and teacher lectures, a

computer design center, desktop editing capabilities, and other resources for researching aspects of theatre, such as dialect, costumes, historical events or periods, music, plays, and literature. Equipment should include compact-disc players and monitors, video camera, tripod, videocassette recorders, and television monitors.

The theatre or auditorium should be a facility designed for the presentation of plays and musicals and should have stage-lighting and audio systems. The following service areas need to be available for all theatre facilities:

- Construction area, with a secure area for storing tools for building sets and equipment for painting and decorating sets

- Storage area for furniture, costumes, props, set pieces, drapes, drops, cycloramas, and makeup

- Costume construction area, with a sewing machine, an iron and ironing board, and storage for sewing and designing tools

- Dressing rooms for male and female students, with showers, toilets, and several lighted mirror stations for applying makeup

Goals for Theatre Education

Artistic Perception Component

Goal 1. *Students observe the environment and respond, using movement and voice.*

Goal 2. *Students observe informal productions, theatrical productions, films, and electronic media and respond to them, using the vocabulary and language of the theatre.*

Creative Expression Component

Goal 3. *Students develop knowledge and skills in acting and directing through their own experience and imagination as well as through their research of literature and history.*

Goal 4. *Students explore the elements and technology of theatrical production through varied media.*

Goal 5. *Students write scripts based on experience, heritage, imagination, literature, and history.*

Historical and Cultural Context Component

Goal 6. *Students research relationships between theatre, history, and culture.*

Goal 7. *Students investigate major themes and historical periods and styles of theatre in different cultures.*

Aesthetic Valuing Component

Goal 8. *Students develop and use criteria for judging and evaluating informal productions, formal productions, films, and electronic media.*

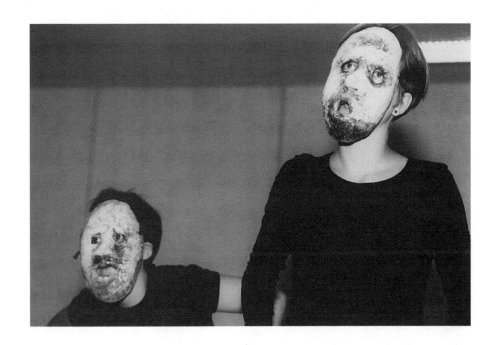

Artistic Perception Component

 Goal 1. *Students observe the environment and respond, using movement and voice.*

Examples of Knowledge and Skills for Goal 1

Kindergarten Through Grade Four	Grades Five Through Eight	Grades Nine Through Twelve Proficient	Grades Nine Through Twelve Advanced
Students use their bodies to move as objects, animals, or people they have observed.	Students clarify and refine movements that specify objects, animals, or people.	Students isolate and refine spatial qualities that affect characterization.	Student actors explore the use of body language to convey surroundings.
Students listen to and reproduce sounds of animate and inanimate objects, animals, and people.	Students use their voices to convey mood, character, and emotion in recounting personal experiences and stories.	Students perform scripts in which all action is communicated solely through the voice.	Student actors perform original, printed scripts in which characterization and action is communicated through the voice.

 Goal 2. *Students observe informal productions, theatrical productions, films, and electronic media and respond to them, using the vocabulary and language of the theatre.*

Examples of Knowledge and Skills for Goal 2

Students observe and recall performances by students and visiting artists from various cultures.	Students document observations and perceptions of performances through reflective journals.	Students adapt observations and perceptions of performances for use in their own creations, either scripted or improvised.	Student actors demonstrate their analyses of the performances of other artists by writing a critique of a film or play performance.
Students describe production values (e.g., lighting, mood, color, atmosphere, and sound) and their impact on emotion.	Students document observations and perceptions of production values through reflective journals.	Students demonstrate their understanding of production values by making annotations on a script written for class.	Student directors view and identify works by the same playwright, director, or designer or works produced in the same style and critique the works through essays or class discussion.

Creative Expression Component

 Goal 3. *Students develop knowledge and skills in acting and directing through their own experience and imagination as well as through their research of literature and history.*

Examples of Knowledge and Skills for Goal 3

Kindergarten Through Grade Four	Grades Five Through Eight	Grades Nine Through Twelve Proficient	Grades Nine Through Twelve Advanced
Students convey the emotional qualities of given characters through simple dramatizations.	Students perform scenes and plays that provide a wide range of characters with varied speech and movement patterns.	Students perform scenes or plays from a varied repertoire, demonstrating voices, dialects, and body movements of a variety of characters.	Student actors research a character from a traditional play, Western or non-Western, and perform a monologue by the character, using appropriate cultural and historical dialect and body movement.
Students collaboratively plan and perform simple improvisations, scenes, or plays, using various ways of staging classroom dramatizations.	Students identify and demonstrate interpretations of scripts and production choices; work in small groups to plan and rehearse scenes; and explore the interrelated responsibilities involved in production.	Students experiment with the elements of directorial choices, comparing production and script interpretation ideas through the use of research, reflection, and dialogue. Students demonstrate specific interpretations and organize rehearsals for informal or formal productions.	Students research a script, justify selections of text and other directorial choices, and work collaboratively to meet the goals of an informal or formal production.

 Goal 4. *Students explore the elements and technology of theatrical production through varied media.*

Examples of Knowledge and Skills for Goal 4

Kindergarten Through Grade Four	Grades Five Through Eight	Grades Nine Through Twelve Proficient	Grades Nine Through Twelve Advanced
Students use simple costume pieces to encourage experimentation and provide stimuli for characterization.	Students choose costumes and create simple props for use in a given play set in a specific time period.	Students research cultural and period dress for use with a particular dramatic text drawn from a specific world culture.	Student designers research and design costumes and props for a play, considering such elements as environment, period, character, and intent.

Examples of Knowledge and Skills for Goal 4 *(Continued)*

Kindergarten Through Grade Four	Grades Five Through Eight	Grades Nine Through Twelve Proficient	Grades Nine Through Twelve Advanced
Students create settings for dramatic play, using available materials.	Students acquire a working knowledge of basic set construction terminology, through demonstration and practice, by building model set designs and drawing renditions of sets.	Students learn the principles of scale, perspective, and architectural drawing in order to design a stage set for a particular play.	Students design sets for a particular play, considering such elements as environment, period, mood, and intent.

 Goal 5. *Students write scripts based on experience, heritage, imagination, literature, and history.*

Examples of Knowledge and Skills for Goal 5

Students retell and dramatically improvise a story.	Students research a given time period and write a script—beginning, conflict, resolution, ending—set in that period.	Students research a specific style of plays; then write and refine a script, focusing on characterization, motivation, environment.	Student writers research the plays of a given dramatist and critique that writer's use of exposition, complication, and crisis in three or more works.
Students create and perform a structured improvisation; evaluate it; then replay the piece.	Students write scenes or short one-act plays, including dialogue, action, and scenic elements.	Students critique, through reflective journals or essays, informal and formal scripts for theatre, film, and other dramatic media.	Student writers write a work in the style of a particular playwright or director.

Historical and Cultural Context Component

Goal 6. *Students research relationships between theatre, history, and culture.*

Examples of Knowledge and Skills for Goal 6

Kindergarten Through Grade Four	Grades Five Through Eight	Grades Nine Through Twelve Proficient	Grades Nine Through Twelve Advanced
Students view and participate in activities, such as storytelling, puppetry, improvisation, and plays, representing various cultures and languages.	Students demonstrate, through dramatic adaptations of cultural stories, an understanding of dramatic literature and performance in the context of time and culture.	Students analyze, through discussion and essays, theatrical styles, themes, or works of authors that define various times and cultures.	Students analyze and adapt, through discussion and projects, theatrical styles, themes, or works of authors that define another time and culture.
Students describe theatrical and film productions representing various cultures and languages.	Students analyze, through class discussion and essays, theatrical, film, and electronic media presentations from a variety of cultures.	Students assess, through research and reflective journals, the cultural effects of various media.	Students research information about specific theatre venues and the actor-audience relationship of a period or culture.

Goal 7. *Students investigate major themes and historical periods and styles of theatre in different cultures.*

Examples of Knowledge and Skills for Goal 7

Students develop a basic understanding of the origins of theatre through viewing, discussing, and acting in or improvising stories, fairy tales, myths, and folklore of various cultures.	Students read, explore, and perform drama from a variety of cultures to expand their knowledge of theatre literature.	Students read, explore, and perform scenes or plays reflecting specific historical and contemporary contexts.	Students research the background, styles, period, and historical and cultural contexts of a given play.
Students use folklore for creative classroom dramatic play.	Students demonstrate knowledge of theatrical history in various cultures by researching and performing folklore from a variety of cultures.	Students analyze the relationship of changes in theatre (e.g., acting, design, architecture, technology, and theme) to societal changes in various cultures.	Student actors trace specific themes across a variety of theatrical works from various historical and contemporary cultures and perform skits or scenes.

Aesthetic Valuing Component

Goal 8. *Students develop and use criteria for judging and evaluating informal productions, formal productions, films, and electronic media.*

Examples of Knowledge and Skills for Goal 8

Students discuss the use of basic acting terminology, such as projection and vocal and physical characterization of self and others.	Students use the basic terminology of evaluation (e.g., intent, structure, effectiveness, and worth) when critiquing their own and others' performances.	Students apply the terminology of evaluation in drawing conclusions about the quality of works read or seen.	Students compare and contrast a variety of dramatic literature, using appropriate evaluation criteria and terminology.
Students discuss the successful use of basic playwriting techniques, such as character, structure, and style.	Students participate in self-evaluation, using a rubric, open-ended questions, and reflective journals; noting effective elements; and making suggestions for improvement.	Students develop criteria for exploring the contributions to meaning of all the elements, individually and in concert, of a production.	Student actors discuss or defend the merits of alternative interpretations of the same work of a given dramatist.

Glossary: The Language of Theatre

acting. The process by which an individual uses the entire self—body, mind, voice, and emotions—to interpret and perform the role of an imagined or assumed character.

action. The core of a theatre piece; the sense of forward movement created by the sequence of events and the physical and psychological motivations of characters.

apron. The area of the stage that extends toward the audience, in front of the main curtain; it is often used as a playing area.

blocking. The positions and movements throughout the play that are designed and planned by the director to focus the audience's attention on the important place or person during every moment of the play.

character. The role played by an actor as he or she assumes another's identity—physically, mentally, and emotionally.

conflict. The problem or incident that creates the action and is resolved by the end of the play. There are only three kinds of conflicts: human versus human, human versus self, and human versus circumstances or environment.

creative drama. An improvisational, nonexhibition, process-centered form of drama in which participants are guided by a leader to imagine, enact, and reflect human experiences.

dialogue. The words spoken by the actors in a drama.

dramatic media. The means of telling stories, through stage, film, television, radio, or computers.

elements of theatre. The individual components used to create and talk about works of theatre. Components include *character, dialogue, music, plot,* and *theme* (see individual entries listed in alphabetical order).

ensemble. A group of actors able to play many parts in a theatrical production; a cast of actors able to work together effectively to present a theatrical production.

formal production. The staging of a theatrical work for presentation before an audience.

improvisation. The spontaneous use of movement and speech to create a character in a particular situation, usually without a script.

informal production. The exploration of all aspects of a theatrical work (such as visual, oral, aural) in a setting in which experimentation is emphasized.

literacy. An understanding of and facility with the concepts and language of the theatre.

plot. The "what happens" in a story: the beginning, which involves the setting, the characters, and the problem they are facing; the middle, which tells how the characters work to solve the problem; and the ending, in which the problem is resolved.

proscenium arch. A decorative arch that separates the stage from the audience.

proscenium opening. The opening framed by the proscenium arch.

script. The written dialogue, description, and directions provided by the playwright.

setting. The locale or locales of the action of the play.

stage. Any place used for presenting shows to an audience, such as the following:

arena stage—The stage is in the center of the audience.

proscenium stage—The stage is framed by the proscenium.

thrust stage—The audience is on three sides of the stage.

stagecraft. The knowledge and skills required to create the physical aspects of a production (e.g., scenery, properties, lights, sound).

storyboard. A graphic, visual outline of the course of action in an improvisation, a play, a film, or a television drama.

style. There are two major styles of theatre. One is presentational, in which the story is offered directly to the audience with no attempt to re-create reality. An example of this style is *A Midsummer Night's Dream,* by Shakespeare. In the second the story is enacted as though it were real and the audience views it through an imaginary fourth wall. Examples are *A Christmas Carol,* by Charles Dickens; and *The Diary of Anne Frank,* by Frances Goodrich and Albert Hackett. *Note:* In some contemporary theatre the two styles are mixed.

theatre. Art that is focused toward the audience; it includes activities, such as acting, directing, designing, managing, and performing other technical tasks, leading to the formal presentation of a scripted play.

theme. The central thought, idea, or significance of the action with which a play or story deals.

types of theatre. Particular kinds of theatre, based on Aristotle's *Poetics:*

tragedy—A play in which the protagonist (leading character) is ultimately defeated or dies. Examples of tragedy are *Romeo and Juliet,* by Shakespeare; and *Oedipus Rex,* by Sophocles.

comedy—A play that is humorous in its treatment of theme and generally has a happy ending in which the protagonist is ultimately victorious.

melodrama—A division of comedy characterized by a serious or dangerous situation in which the protagonist finally wins. Examples of melodrama are found in various detective and Western stories.

farce—A division of comedy in which situations and characters are exaggerated to create humor and in which the protagonist wins and survives. Examples of farce include *Twelfth Night,* by Shakespeare; the television series *I Love Lucy;* and many other situation comedies on television.

wings. A series of flats or drapes hung on both sides of the stage, parallel to the proscenium frame, often accompanied by a painted backdrop depicting a scene; the space off-stage masked by the drapes. Wings may be used for exits and entrances.

Chapter 6

Visual Arts

There is nothing in art that there wasn't some of before.

—David Smith (1906–1965)

The visual arts have been a part of human expression since prehistoric times, beginning with the images painted and scratched on cave walls through contemporary, cross-cultural, collaborative public installations. The visual arts have been used in all cultures and civilizations to communicate ideas, customs, traditions, and beliefs. The value of instruction and exposure to the visual arts is immeasurable in the humanizing process.

Through the visual arts images become a part of human language. For example, the marks made by young children are a part of their first attempts at language. The visual arts build on a child's natural inclination to communicate beyond those first marks.

The visual arts consist of two-dimensional and three-dimensional creative expressions, such as painting, drawing, graphic arts, printmaking, sculpture, photography, ceramics, architecture, product design and commercial art, textile, and fiber arts. Also included are forms that combine many media, such as performances, installations, environmental art, site-specific works, and multimedia pieces.

Education using the visual arts includes developing the perception essential to visual arts; acquiring skills in creative expression in visual arts media for the sake of the art itself and for informed appreciation; studying the cultural and social history of civilizations, as reflected in the artworks of a people; and developing skills in aesthetics to make critical judgments of artworks. Emphasis is also placed on cross-cultural studies of common art forms and the distinguishing characteristics and history of works of art.

Visual arts students are exposed to a variety of art forms from authentic sources whenever possible. Instruction includes exploring processes for reflection on and analysis of artworks so that students understand the power of works of art and the sources of inspiration of those works; researching the historical and cultural connections of artworks; and experimenting with processes and techniques used in the creation of artworks. A primary goal is to assist students in understanding the creativity of others as well as their own by emphasizing the creative process and the product. Through a carefully structured visual arts program, beginning at the kindergarten level, students develop their personal artistic style and vision.

The visual arts have played a major role in recording the customs, history, and artistic values of civilizations. Knowledge of that role enhances and deepens students' understanding in other core curricular areas. A comprehensive, well-planned art program provides opportunities for students to develop and use the language of the arts and to perceive and understand aesthetic concepts, giving students a foundation for aesthetic valuing and criticism.

A visual arts program needs to:

1. Be well planned and developmentally appropriate, from kindergarten through grade twelve.

2. Provide opportunities for guided reflection about and analysis of artworks.

3. Provide opportunities for personal skill development, with emphasis on the creative process as well as the product.

4. Develop informed citizens with a lifelong commitment to the arts.

5. Develop students' appreciation for and understanding of the artworks of many cultures and periods in world history.

The Four Components of Visual Arts Education

Effective visual arts instruction incorporates all four arts components: artistic perception, creative expression, historical and cultural context, and aesthetic valuing. An effective

visual arts teacher understands that for students to create artworks, they must see and respond to works of art in ways that enable them to understand the power and nature of aesthetic experience. Students also need to experience the visual arts of a variety of cultures and from many historical periods.

Artistic Perception

Developing an understanding of the visual characteristics of artworks, other objects made by humans, nature, and the events people experience requires the use of the senses of sight, smell, sound, and touch. The ways in which people perceive are shaped by their individual experiences and the opportunities they have to educate their senses. Students learn to recognize the visual structures and functions of art through the observation, comprehension, and application of composition and design principles. Perceiving and understanding the components of the visual arts requires an awareness and comprehension of the language of the visual arts.

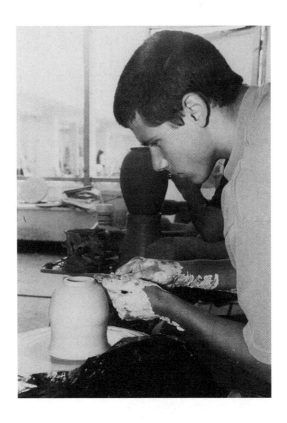

Creative Expression

Expression in the visual arts includes the creation and performance of original works of art and involves the interpretation of thoughts, perceptions, and ideas in creating artworks. Students must actively work in these expressive modes to understand and appreciate the visual arts. Students recognize the importance of respecting the originality of their own visual expressions and the artwork of others and of understanding the variety of media and technical proficiency used in works of art. Students develop visual arts skills and increase their visual literacy by using a variety of media and technical processes. Creative expression in the visual arts helps students know themselves better and appreciate their own and others' creativity.

All painting is a kind of talking about life.

—Romare Bearden (1912–1988)

Historical and Cultural Context

Through the study of visual arts from a variety of cultures, students gain an understanding and appreciation of the creative expression of people across time and place. They understand the role and social context of the visual arts and artists and the significance of the visual arts within world cultures. Students also understand the historical development of the visual arts in the United States and are able to place their own work in its historical and cultural context.

Aesthetic Valuing

Analyzing and responding to their own artworks and to those of others allows students to understand the feelings and ideas expressed in two-dimensional and three-dimensional works of art created by artists of many cultures, places, and times.

Aesthetic valuing in the visual arts involves analysis of and appreciative response to the intent, purpose, and technical proficiency of artworks. Students learn to make sound critical judgments about the quality and success of artworks from their own experiences in and perceptions about the visual arts. They express their responses through discussion and written forms.

Curriculum and Instruction in Visual Arts Education

Effective visual arts instruction calls for regular, planned, and cumulative learning opportunities beginning in preschool and continuing through high school, with expanding content and diverse instructional strategies. A plan for systematic student assessment and program evaluation also needs to be designed as a part of the curriculum.

It is important to provide appropriate facilities, equipment, and materials for creating and studying the visual arts. These provisions allow students to explore ideas and media; promote innovative thinking; and enable students to experience creating and contemplating original works of art. The use of technology also needs to be an integral part of the visual arts curriculum.

Elementary School

All students in California elementary schools need to be involved in a carefully designed and implemented visual arts program that provides opportunities for developing knowledge of and skills in the visual arts, an appreciation of art, and an understanding of the historical and cultural aspects and value of the visual arts. Whenever possible, classroom teachers should plan and initiate a complete program in visual arts together with a visual arts specialist.

Students in elementary schools need to be able to identify a variety of artworks from many periods and cultures. They are introduced to, and practice using, the language of the visual arts in discussions of artworks. Instruction helps students understand the historical and cultural contexts of works of art, styles and periods of art, and cultural group expressions. In addition, students in the elementary school need to have opportunities to identify and discuss the characteristics of master works of art. This process enables students to learn about their own responses to works of art and to assess those responses in light of the observed art.

In placing the emphasis on the creative process, the elementary school visual arts curriculum provides opportunities for students to accept their own creative and original expressions. As students discuss and understand their own expressions, they develop an understanding of the works of others. The elementary school visual arts program gives young artists opportunities to explore and experience the visual arts, using a wide variety of art media.

Middle School

The middle school visual arts program extends the elementary school learning and experience in the visual arts and prepares students for specialization in high school art classes. A comprehensive middle school visual arts curriculum enables all students to acquire knowledge of the visual arts, develop artistic skills, and expand their creative potential in the visual arts. It promotes lifelong involvement in and appreciation of the arts.

Middle schools provide visual arts instruction in exploratory, elective, and special-interest classes. Visual arts instruction is also included during arts-infused interdisciplinary and thematic-based instruction in core curriculum classes, such as English–language arts and history. Visual arts instruction in the middle grades is related to the developmental

Visual Arts: A Closer Look at History

Sixth-grade students studying the ancient civilization of Egypt conduct research about the Egyptian kings, particularly Pharaoh Tutankhamen. They investigate the uses of the king's power and the reasons for including a variety of objects in the king's tomb. Were the objects symbolic of the king's power? Were there individual portraits of the king? What did the paintings in the tomb mean? What is the geography of the region in which the tomb is located? What did this have to do with the construction of the tomb itself? Other topics that could be researched include the clothing of the time and its relationship to rank; the significance of various creatures depicted on walls and funerary masks; and the reason for recording in tomb paintings the labor of the lower classes as well as festive occasions for the nobility.

Afterwards, the students construct displays focused on the results of their research. In addition to the written essays, these displays might include clay masks similar to those made by the king's craftsmen; diagrams showing the location of the tomb and topography of the region; and drawings or illustrations of individual scenes in the life of the king. (Refer to the visual arts color center section to see a photo of Pharaoh Tutankhamen and for more examples of connections between the visual arts and history–social science.)

stages and interests of the young adolescent. Instruction includes experiences for individual students or collaborating groups of students. The young adolescent often assists in the definition of the artistic problem.

Middle school students need to compile portfolios, which are sometimes maintained on a CD-ROM or another form of technology.

High School

The high school visual arts program is an integral part of the school's visual and performing arts department. Visual arts students in high school begin in-depth studies in one or more areas of concentration or elect to investigate a broad base of arts knowledge and skills.

Students need to be provided with a variety of learning opportunities in two-dimensional and three-dimensional media, at beginning, intermediate, and advanced levels, that progress to innovative and challenging experiences. Creative thinking in the four components of artistic perception, creative expression, cultural and historical context, and aesthetic valuing needs to be promoted through a series of appropriate introductory and advanced visual arts courses. Connections of the visual arts to other curriculum areas expand and enhance the scope of the student's educational experience.

A part of the high school visual arts program is also devoted to investigations of human responses—the responses of students and others—to artworks. This aspect enables students to explore the nature and components of aesthetic experience.

High school students need to create portfolios to track their individual growth, prepare for high school exit, apply for college entrance and scholarships, or obtain employment in the visual arts.

Students with Special Needs

All students can and need to participate in a visual arts program that provides a context in which they can make meaning through exploration, interaction, risk taking, assessment, reflection, and refinement of their experiences.

In the visual arts all students are constantly exploring their individual limitations and their creative gifts. The multifaceted nature of the visual arts allows all students to find their own interests and strengths, whether through painting, drawing, graphic arts, printmaking, sculpture, photography, ceramics, textile, or fiber arts. The teacher encourages students to push the boundaries of their abilities.

Students at risk of dropping out of school, who may not show interest in other subject areas, often find success in visual arts classes in which they can express themselves safely. With peer and teacher support, visual arts programs provide a creative outlet and an opportunity for reflection so that students at risk of dropping out build self-esteem, make meaningful friendships, strengthen their support systems, and understand connections to other core disciplines, thus enhancing their interest in school.

Lessons can be adapted for visually impaired students. Sculpture can be used for those who are blind and magnification devices in computer and video technology for students with low vision.

Student Exhibitions

Student art exhibitions allow students to share their work and visual arts experiences

with peers and adults. Exhibited work needs to include examples of works in progress in addition to finished pieces.

The exhibit, whether in the classroom, school, or community, needs to make clear to the viewer that student artworks are on display. Statements that provide amplification of the work are often included with each displayed artwork. Examples of these statements are descriptions of the assignment, the student's intentions, or challenges encountered by the student. Often, photographs of the students at work help clarify the context of the artworks on exhibit.

The purpose of an exhibition of student artworks is to demonstrate variety in what students are doing in their visual arts classrooms. This intention is consistently emphasized in the publicity and organization of the exhibit; the commentary on wall statements or in programs; and the thoughtful arrangement of the artworks.

Assessment in Visual Arts Education

Assessment in the visual arts focuses students' and teachers' attention on the inseparability of assessment and instruction. As indicated in Chapter 2, assessment becomes instruction when students and teachers reflect together on content standards or expectations of achievement and discuss ways of achieving those standards.

Wolf and Pistone enumerate five assumptions about the efficacy of assessment in the arts. First, both students and teachers insist on excellence of learning as exhibited in performance. High standards are set, and studio and classroom discussions involve ways in which to reach those standards. Second, there is much talk on judgment—opinions on a range of qualitative issues—and decisions based on insight, reason, and craft. Third, self-assessment is important for all artists. Students need to learn how to

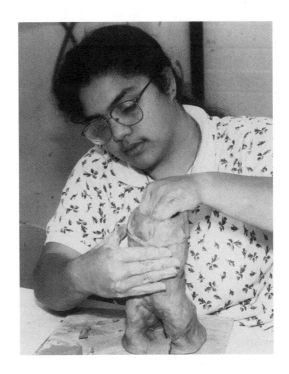

understand and appraise their own work as well as that of their peers and other visual artists. Fourth, varied forms of assessment need to be used to obtain information about both individual and group performances. These forms are discussed in Chapter 2 and include everyday conversation and comments, critiques, and reviews. Fifth, ongoing assessment allows students to reflect on their own creations and use the insights gained from the process to enrich their work. Viewed in this way, assessment is an episode of learning.[1]

Wolf and her colleagues, who developed the handbook titled *Arts Propel: A Handbook for Visual Arts,* make an assumption that "ongoing assessment, both formal and informal, by students themselves and by teachers (in effect a dialogue about work and ways of working), yields revealing profiles of development and promotes learning and new levels of achievement."[2] For example,

---

[1] D. P. Wolf and N. Pistone, *Taking Full Measure: Rethinking Assessment Through the Arts.* New York: College Entrance Examination Board, 1991.

[2] *Arts Propel: A Handbook for Visual Arts.* Edited by Ellen Winner. Cambridge, Mass.: Educational Testing Service and Harvard Project Zero, 1992.

through active involvement with art materials, students are engaged in the process of making art and in artistic problems. Connecting creation, perception, and reflection stimulates students to think about how artists, their peers, and artists from other times and cultures have confronted similar issues. This process involves assessing work regularly while in progress and at the end of the project.

The following example illustrates the ways in which assessment directs student effort so that the result is satisfying to the teacher and student alike:

In a high school visual arts classroom, the teacher always incorporates into the curriculum a written component consisting of gallery reviews. Students begin the unit of study by looking at a group of prints and learning the appropriate vocabulary for describing materials, techniques, and aesthetic qualities. Then they write reviews of books or reports on artists, using the appropriate vocabulary and putting the artists into the appropriate context.

In preparation for the gallery review, the teacher presents slides of the various art galleries in the area and helps students to understand the availability of visual art in their area.

Finally, students visit a gallery or museum or attend an art event or activity and write reviews of the exhibits. A list of questions to be addressed is supplied for reference.

Other gallery reviews are assigned, including a review of the annual student art exhibition.

The teacher scores each student's gallery reviews separately and considers the body of work as a portfolio. The teacher may elicit students' ideas about suitable criteria for judging artworks. In this way

students think about what might be expected of them for a series of gallery reviews.[3]

The Role of Technology in Visual Arts Education

The goal for using technology in visual arts education is to provide all students with additional ways in which to communicate about and within the arts, to create artworks and express ideas artistically, and to understand and appreciate the arts. The challenge to visual arts educators is to offer students opportunities to use combinations of old and contemporary technologies for creative expression. Electronic technologies facilitate learning about the historical and cultural context and development of the visual arts. The technologies may also assist students in learning about issues related to criticism and valuation of visual arts.

Advances in electronic technologies, such as laser discs, hypercard, interactive computer-videos, art and design software, desktop publishing, and visual databases, are now affordable and available for use in schools. CD-ROMs, the Internet, and the World Wide Web (WWW) provide burgeoning access not only to technical information but also to visual arts information, exhibitions, museum collections, multimedia presentations, communication, journal critiques, and reviews that suggest strategies for the use of the visual arts in the classroom.

Using technology for assessment is one of the most valuable applications for visual arts teachers. Recording students' work on

---

[3] This example of assessment in the visual arts is adapted from one devised by Jack Haehl, a teacher in the San Rafael Unified School District. It is found in *Prelude to Performance Assessment in the Arts, Kindergarten Through Grade Twelve.* Sacramento: California Department of Education, 1993, pp. 40–41.

videotape permits students to evaluate and reflect on their own work. Video portfolios can be economically duplicated, transferred to CD-ROM, stored, and shared with others. In the process students develop a sense of history, an awareness of a common past, and a sense of accomplishment.

The implications of technology for visual arts education are both challenging and profound: challenging because technology needs to support student learning and enhance the fundamental knowledge and skills of students in one or more forms of the visual arts; profound because technology provides visual arts educators with an immense amount of information and resources. Access to visual databases in museums, such as the National Gallery of Art in Washington, D.C., provides teachers with instant access to images by master artists. Students also have the opportunity to enhance their learning through their own research in these databases.

Teacher Preparation and Professional Development

Teachers are best prepared to teach the visual arts when they have a strong foundation in the knowledge and skills required to create and respond to artworks in two and three dimensions and in multimedia. In addition, the inclusion of aesthetics, art history, and art criticism in the core of classes that prospective teachers take would enable them to discuss artworks from a variety of viewpoints. Each potential visual arts teacher needs to have a diverse background in the visual arts, including course work that enables the teacher to communicate the historical and cultural foundations of the visual arts, and an area of specialization. Teacher education institutions need to allow for and encourage this diversity and recognize that a combination of art experiences is critical to the artistic progress of artists and teachers.

School districts are encouraged to support visual arts coordinators and to provide for teachers' continual professional growth in the visual arts. Teachers need to be encouraged to enroll in visual arts courses in local colleges and universities and be allowed opportunities to participate in special workshops offered by their professional organization in the visual arts.

Teachers of the visual arts need to be able to provide an environment that fosters students' love of creation. This objective can be achieved principally when teachers know and teach the fundamental principles of the visual arts, including teaching students to observe and reflect on master works of art, their own work, and that of their peers. Students need to explore a variety of ideas and media in a nurturing atmosphere that encourages experimentation and risk. In addition, students need to know how to improve their knowledge and skills in the visual arts by assessing their achievement, using various forms of performance-based assessment.

Visual arts teachers at the middle and high school levels should be able to structure and teach specialized visual arts technique classes appropriate to students' skill levels, needs, and interests. At those levels teachers also need to be able to recognize interested and talented visual art students and challenge them, through referrals to other special learning environments and opportunities, to expand their talents.

Professional development can occur through workshops with peers; demonstrations or exchanged classroom visits; coaching and mentoring by district and county office specialists or artists; courses at institutions of higher education to perfect or expand on artistic endeavors; studies at museums; participation in meetings and conferences of state and national arts and educational professional organizations and agencies; and institutes and workshops, such as those offered by The California Arts Project (TCAP). It is essential for schools and districts to support teachers' lifelong learning in the visual arts with released time and funding.

Resources, Environment, Materials, and Equipment

A well-designed learning environment enhances the visual arts program in elementary, middle, and high schools. The facility is designed aesthetically and provides adequate, uncrowded space in which students can work on a variety of art experiences. The art room provides storage space for materials, equipment, and student works in progress.

Special safety, energy, lighting, location, sound control, and maintenance needs must be considered. And access to the facility by students with physical disabilities and students with exceptional needs must be ensured. Space for display and exhibition of two-dimensional and three-dimensional artworks needs to be available to students and accessible by the whole school population for viewing of the artworks.

Safety issues are important in visual arts education. A clean environment is essential for health and safety. Ventilation must be adequate to exhaust all fumes, dust, or odors.

Program Advisory CIL: 94/95-01, issued on July 12, 1994, provides all elementary, middle, and secondary school personnel with information on legislation regulating the purchase of art and craft materials and guide-lines for the safe use of the materials.[4] The appendix to the advisory contains a list titled "Art and Craft Materials Which Cannot Be Purchased for Use in Kindergarten and Grades One Through Six."

The advisory informs school personnel about precautions to be taken when purchasing materials for use in grades seven through twelve. *Education Code* Section 32064 mandates labeling standards for art and craft materials purchased for grades seven through twelve when those materials contain toxic substances. The regulation is predicated on the assumption that students in grades seven through twelve are capable of reading and understanding warning labels on art products and, once aware of the hazard, can take the necessary precautions to minimize exposure to the hazard. This assumption makes it incumbent on teachers to ensure that all students in grades seven through twelve are aware of hazardous materials and resources and know the steps to be taken should they become exposed to those materials. Although not mandated by law for this grade span, purchasing products that do not contain toxic ingredients will provide an additional measure of safety in the classroom.

Materials most often found on restricted lists include glues, paints, ceramic glazes, dyes, painting mediums, and cleaning solvents. Teachers are advised to be aware of safety hazards, to examine labels, and to follow instructions for the safe use of materials.

The tools and equipment used in design-craft classes, jewelry classes, and most classes in additive and subtractive sculpture require instruction in safety. Safety examinations should be given regularly to students and the results kept on file. Safety goggles, dust masks, and sight and hearing protectors must be worn when working with selected materials and equipment, such as toxic dyes, air brushes, spray-glaze equipment, loud drills, and band saws.

---

[4] This program advisory is available from the California Department of Education, Middle School Curriculum Office; telephone (916) 654-5979.

Goals for Visual Arts Education

Artistic Perception Component

Goal 1. *Students use their senses to perceive works of art, objects in nature, events, and the environment.*

Goal 2. *Students identify visual structures and functions of art, using the language of the visual arts.*

Creative Expression Component

Goal 3. *Students develop knowledge of and artistic skills in a variety of visual arts media and technical processes.*

Goal 4. *Students create original artworks based on personal experiences or responses.*

Goal 5. *Students develop skills in the visual arts and appreciation for using the visual arts in lifelong learning.*

Historical and Cultural Context Component

Goal 6. *Students explore the role of the visual arts in culture and human history.*

Goal 7. *Students investigate major themes in historical and contemporary periods and styles of the visual arts throughout the world.*

Aesthetic Valuing Component

Goal 8. *Students derive meaning from artworks through analysis, interpretation, and judgment.*

Artistic Perception Component

Goal 1. *Students use their senses to perceive works of art, objects in nature, events, and the environment.*

Examples of Knowledge and Skills for Goal 1

Kindergarten Through Grade Four	Grades Five Through Eight	Grades Nine Through Twelve Proficient	Grades Nine Through Twelve Advanced
Students use symbols to reflect understanding of visual characteristics of the world environment.	Students observe and record visual and tactile qualities of the physical world and use those observations in artwork.	Students perceive their surroundings and demonstrate the relationship of their visual experience to their ability to create original works of art.	Student artists create works that demonstrate their observations and perceptions of the visual characteristics of the world.
Students use imaginative techniques and methods to illustrate what they see in the natural world.	Students use a variety of techniques and media to illustrate their observations of the environment.	Students demonstrate, through essays and class discussion, their understanding of the elements of design in nature and in artworks based on nature.	Student artists create works of art in two dimensions and three dimensions based on their own written descriptions of the natural or human environment.

Goal 2. *Students identify visual structures and functions of art, using the language of the visual arts.*

Examples of Knowledge and Skills for Goal 2

Students learn the language of the visual arts, such as the elements of art and principles of design, through discussions of master works of art.	Students expand their visual arts vocabulary as they observe and use the elements and principles of design in language and visual imagery.	Students comprehend the aesthetics of perception and demonstrate their application, extension, and creative use of the visual arts vocabulary in essays and discussion.	Student artists analyze aesthetic qualities of their own artworks and the works of others and refine their own works.
Students discuss works of art, using the vocabulary of the visual arts.	Students recognize visual structures in art and understand how to record their impressions in their own artworks.	Students discriminate among a variety of visual structures and functions to perceive commonalities and differences and describe these in essays and class discussion.	Student artists analyze and synthesize the underlying structures and functions of the environment and events and apply a high level of original thinking to produce artworks.

Creative Expression Component

Goal 3. *Students develop knowledge of and artistic skills in a variety of visual arts media and technical processes.*

Examples of Knowledge and Skills for Goal 3

Kindergarten Through Grade Four	Grades Five Through Eight	Grades Nine Through Twelve Proficient	Grades Nine Through Twelve Advanced
Students identify elements and principles of design that appear in their own artworks.	Students demonstrate, through their creations, combinations of elements and principles of design.	Students create works of visual art that demonstrate an understanding of the power of the elements and principles of design.	Student artists use the elements and principles of design in technically proficient and intuitive ways across a variety of media.
Students use a variety of two- and three-dimensional media on different surfaces to communicate ideas and feelings.	Students identify two- and three-dimensional media and use them to create visual images that communicate ideas.	Students create unique artworks, using the characteristics of two- and three-dimensional media, and apply technical skills to communicate effectively.	Student artists initiate, define, and solve challenging visual arts problems in two- and three-dimensional media, using such intellectual skills as analysis, synthesis, and evaluation.

Goal 4. *Students create original artworks based on personal experiences or responses.*

Examples of Knowledge and Skills for Goal 4

Kindergarten Through Grade Four	Grades Five Through Eight	Grades Nine Through Twelve Proficient	Grades Nine Through Twelve Advanced
Students explore differences among the materials, techniques, and processes used in the visual arts.	Students investigate a variety of media, techniques, and processes that are effective in communicating ideas visually.	Students express their ideas and thoughts through a wide variety of media, techniques, and processes.	Student artists create a series of artworks in a variety of media, communicating specific ideas and intentions from personal experience.
Students combine selected materials and techniques to create a symbol for personal identity.	Students use two-dimensional or three-dimensional media techniques to imbue an inanimate object with personal feelings and characteristics.	Students analyze visual images and recombine them in new and original ways to create a personal statement.	Student artists select specific media and develop a personal study of images that contain and express different meanings.

Goal 5. *Students develop skills in the visual arts and appreciation for using the visual arts in lifelong learning.*

Examples of Knowledge and Skills for Goal 5

Kindergarten Through Grade Four	Grades Five Through Eight	Grades Nine Through Twelve Proficient	Grades Nine Through Twelve Advanced
Students visit an art museum and discuss reasons for placing artworks in special places.	Students use the art museum as a resource for investigating the influences of the visual arts in a community.	Students research the impact of an art museum on a community and write essays on the various festivals and activities supported by the museum.	Students research the roles and backgrounds of museum staff and their decisions in the selection of artworks for exhibit in the museum and report their findings in written and verbal presentations.
Students discuss their responses to their own artworks and to the works of master artists.	Students research different approaches to making critical judgments about works of art.	Students identify different approaches to making critical judgments and use them when reflecting on their own work and that of others.	Students analyze and discuss the ways in which their own work and the works of others use media effectively to translate ideas, feelings, and values into visual statements of aesthetic merit.

Historical and Cultural Context Component

Goal 6. *Students explore the role of the visual arts in culture and human history.*

Examples of Knowledge and Skills for Goal 6

Students recognize a variety of artworks from various cultures.	Students identify artworks from various cultures and understand the way in which the artworks reflect their culture.	Students describe distinguishing characteristics and identifying elements of particular artworks.	Student artists demonstrate an understanding of artworks from a variety of cultures by describing the roles that specific artworks play in those societies.
Students identify the characteristics of art forms from other cultures.	Students identify works of various cultures and determine the ways in which artworks reflect, maintain, and express cultural themes.	Students compare and contrast differences in the expression of common themes and in the use of visual elements, technical processes, and stylistic elements in the artworks of various cultures.	Student artists analyze specific artworks, identify cultural sources, discuss the processes involved, and examine the role of artworks and artists in that society.

Goal 7. *Students investigate major themes in historical and contemporary periods and styles of the visual arts throughout the world.*

Examples of Knowledge and Skills for Goal 7

Kindergarten Through Grade Four	*Grades Five Through Eight*	*Grades Nine Through Twelve Proficient*	*Grades Nine Through Twelve Advanced*
Students identify and discuss the artworks of a particular artist.	Students trace specific ideas through reflective essays about a variety of artworks from all parts of the world.	Students explore a given artist's use of an idea found in a variety of artworks.	Student artists research the use of specific themes and ideas in a variety of cultures throughout the world.
Students read about and discuss artworks from the past and from contemporary times.	Students understand cultural and historical periods and become familiar with the visual arts vocabulary and language of the time.	Students identify and discuss variations in stylistic periods and artistic expressions from different historical eras.	Student artists identify, describe, interpret, and analyze stylistic elements in artworks from the past as well as from contemporary periods.

Aesthetic Valuing Component

Goal 8. *Students derive meaning from artworks through analysis, interpretation, and judgment.*

Examples of Knowledge and Skills for Goal 8

Students discuss the way in which artworks are created.	Students recognize and discuss multiple purposes for creating works of art.	Students respond to visual artworks by discussing and writing about their own interpretations, ideas, attitudes, views, and interactions with artworks.	Through discussion and reflective journal writing, students analyze the variety of reasons for creating artworks and explore the implications of and various purposes for their creation.
Students discuss how experiences influence the development of specific artworks.	Students write essays describing the contemporary and historic meaning in specific artworks.	Through research and small-group discussion, students derive the meaning of specific works and the way in which the works relate to historical and cultural contexts.	Student artists analyze the way in which specific works are created and their relation to historical and cultural contexts.

Glossary: The Language of the Visual Arts

General Terms

abstraction. Art in which the subject matter is stated in a brief, simplified manner, with emphasis on design. Little or no attempt is made to represent forms or subject matter realistically. Uses of abstraction were explored by Wassily Kandinsky in the early twentieth century and were later extended in the works of Pablo Picasso, Jackson Pollock, and Helen Frankenthaler.

aesthetics. A branch of philosophy; the study of art and theories about the nature and components of aesthetic experience.

art criticism. A systematic analysis of a work of art.

art materials. Resources used in the creation and study of visual art; for example, paint, canvas, fiber, charcoal, crayons, wood, clay, film, metal.

composition. The organization of form in a work of art.

design. A comprehensive plan, conception, or organization; the arrangement of independent parts to form a coordinated whole. Formal organization is achieved through the use and interrelationship of the elements and principles of visual art.

emphasis. Special stress given to an element to make it stand out.

figurative. Pertaining to the human figure. Many of the religious paintings by Peter Paul Rubens in the early seventeenth century focus on the human figure, as do the paintings by Edgar Degas in the nineteenth century and those by Alice Neel in the twentieth century.

function. Purpose and use of a work of art.

geometric. Reference to shapes that have uniformly straight or curved edges or surfaces. Piet Mondrian in the early twentieth century was a foremost practitioner of geometric painting to express a philosophic approach to painting. The sculptural work of Tony Smith and Donald Judd in the mid-twentieth century emphasized the nature of pure geometric form, as did the paintings by Frank Stella.

media. Particular categories of art, such as painting, sculpture, film, and video.

medium. Material or technique used to make an artwork.

organic. Reference to shapes having irregular edges or to surfaces resembling things existing in nature.

pattern. Lines, shapes, and colors repeated in a variety of combinations.

positive and negative. Positive shapes in a composition are the solid objects; negative shapes are the unoccupied spaces between positive shapes.

process. A series of actions, changes, or functions that bring about a result.

reflection. Thoughtful consideration of an artwork or aesthetic experience.

structure. The way in which parts are arranged or put together to form a whole; relatively intricate or extensive organization.

style. A set of characteristics of a culture, a period of art, or a school of art; the characteristic expression of an individual artist.

technique. The systematic procedure by which a task is accomplished.

three-dimensional. Reference to qualities of height, width, and depth.

two-dimensional. Reference to qualities of height and width.

Elements of Art

The sensory components used to create and talk about works of art are as follows:

color. The visual sensation dependent on the reflection or absorption of light from a given surface. The three attributes of color are:

hue—The characteristic of color that gives it its name. The spectrum is usually divided into six basic hues: violet, blue, green, yellow, orange, and red.

intensity—The degree of color and brightness or dullness of a color.

value—Lightness and darkness of a hue or neutral color; the gradations of light and dark in a two-dimensional artwork and on the surface of three-dimensional objects.

form. The particular characteristics of an artwork's visual elements, as distinguished from its subject matter or content; a three-dimensional volume with the same qualities as shape; the illusion of three dimensions. Attributes of form are:

mass—Bulk, weight, and density of three-dimensional forms, either actual or implied.

volume—Any three-dimensional quantity that is bound or enclosed, whether solid or void.

line. A point moving in space. It can vary in width, length, and direction.

shape. A two-dimensional area or plane that may be open or closed, free-form or geometric, found in nature or made by humans.

space. The emptiness or area between, around, above, below, or within objects. Shapes and forms are defined by the space around and within them.

texture. The surface quality of materials, either actual (tactile) or implied (visual).

Principles of Design

The controlling, formal organizational concepts in the visual arts are as follows:

balance. The way in which the visual art elements are arranged to create a feeling of equilibrium in an artwork. Examples are:

asymmetry—Intentionally unbalanced parts on opposite sides of a perceived boundary, giving the appearance of equal visual weight.

symmetry—A balance of parts on opposites sides of a perceived boundary; a mirror image.

radial—Lines, shapes, or colors that emanate from a central core.

contrast. Opposites, such as light and dark, rough and smooth, soft and hard, in close proximity.

dominance. The difference in importance or emphasis of one aspect in relation to all other aspects of a design.

dominant. The most prominent principle or the most obvious in influence or position.

emphasis. Special stress given to an element of art to make it stand out.

movement. A way, implied or actual, of causing the eye of the viewer to travel within and across the boundary of a work of art.

repetition. The recurrence of elements of art at regular intervals.

rhythm. Intentional, regular repetition of lines or shapes to achieve a specific effect.

subordination. An element which appears to hold a secondary or lesser importance within a design.

theme and variation. An idea or dominant feature that gives the artwork its character; the subject of a work of art, sometimes with a number of phases or different examples.

unity. Literally, the state of being one. A perception that each part fits, harmonizes, and functions well with everything else in the work.

Chapter 7 *What This Framework Requires of Teachers*

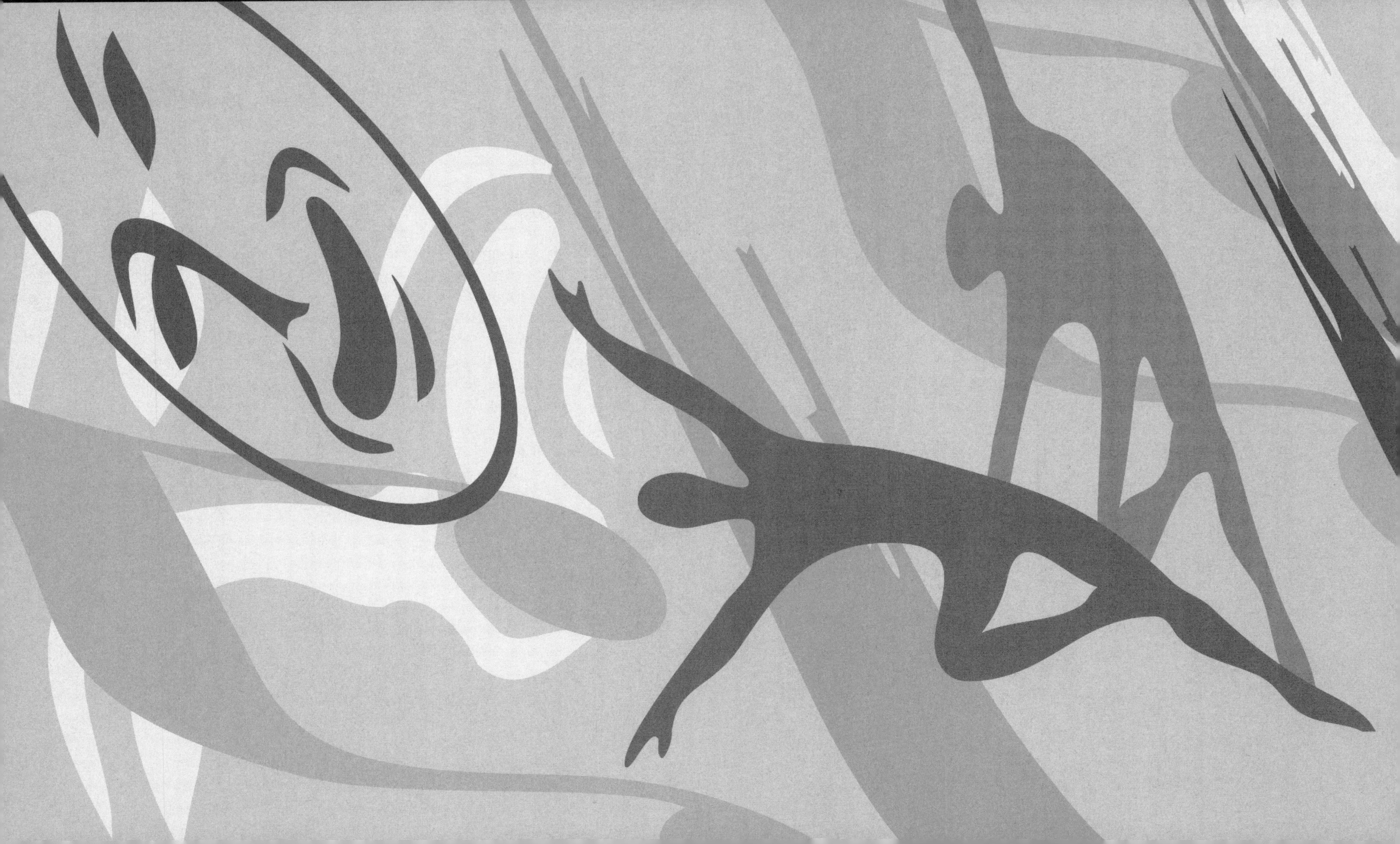

We should find the worlds of knowledge represented in schools by the arts, the humanities, and the sciences equitably balanced and integrated. Young people in America are entitled to an education in which important themes of human purpose are enlivened through the firsthand creations and theories of the world's best minds.

—Brent Wilson, *The Quiet Evolution*

F a vision of a comprehensive arts education for all students at all grades is to be achieved, several capacities for teachers of the arts are critical. These capacities are attained during preservice education and are further developed, refined, and expanded through professional development throughout the teacher's career.

Capacities of Teachers of the Arts

1. **Four arts–four components.** Teachers of the arts understand the four components of the arts—artistic perception, creative expression, historical and cultural context, and aesthetic valuing—and teach the arts from the perspective of the four components.

2. **Interdependence–independence of the arts.** Teachers of the arts understand the interdependence of the arts as well as the independent nature of each arts discipline.

3. **Process and product.** Teachers of the arts focus on arts processes as well as on the arts product or performance.

4. **Affective and cognitive aspects of the arts.** Teachers of the arts understand and develop both the affective and cognitive aspects of the arts.

5. **World arts and cultures.** Teachers of the arts include arts and cultures from many parts of the world in teaching and learning.

6. **Cooperation.** Teachers of the arts work cooperatively with colleagues, members of the arts community, and others responsible for arts education and provide opportunities for students to work and learn cooperatively.

7. **Assessment.** Teachers of the arts design and score arts assessments, using a variety of methods.

8. **Technology.** Teachers of the arts are knowledgeable about and use current electronic technologies.

1. *Four arts–four components.* **Teachers of the arts understand the four components of the arts—artistic perception, creative expression, historical and cultural context, and aesthetic valuing—and teach the arts from the perspective of the four components.**

The curriculum for dance, music, theatre, and the visual arts builds on prior arts experiences. Knowledge and skills are cumulative and allow students continually to construct meaning.

The four components provide the breadth of knowledge and the skills that enable students to experience an arts discipline from varied perspectives. Teachers who have learned an arts discipline as a creator or thoughtful critic are better prepared to teach that art from the perspective of the four components.

For example, the accompanying diagram illustrates the integration of the components in the course of learning about singing. The teacher begins with any component, or segment of the diagram, and moves to any other component. The process is not linear but spatial and often repeats components or segments.

If the teacher begins with the creative expression component by asking students to sing a song in a particular style, the next step might be to explore the historical and cultural context of the song or the relation of that style to the particular tradition in which it is found. What is the unique rhythm structure? In what context was the song composed? For example, in which historic period or place? Who sang the song? For what reasons? Were other songs of a similar nature sung during the same time? What qualities in vocal sound production are specific to the culture?

This exploration might lead to the artistic perception component and an examination of a variety of elements of vocal music examples in ethnic, technical, and stylistic forms. The results of this examination lead the teacher and student into the aesthetic valuing component and a reflective discussion about relationships among the discovered qualities. The reflection takes many forms: students write their observations and perceptions after the discussion, choose songs to sing and give reasons for their selections, or discuss individual songs and the relationships of the rhythms or vocal patterns. The students and teacher may sing the song again, with the new information leading to deeper meaning in the singing.

Artistic Perception Component — Students examine a variety of vocal examples of ethnic, technical, and stylistic forms.

Creative Expression Component — Students sing alone and in rhythm, from memory, a variety of songs representing different genres and styles.

Historical and Cultural Context Component — Students explore the oral traditions of world cultures and their applications to vocal sound production.

Aesthetic Valuing Component — Students discuss the relationships of ethnic, technical, or stylistic forms; choose a selection of songs to sing; and give reasons for their selection.

2. *Interdependence–independence of the arts.* **Teachers of the arts understand the interdependence of the arts as well as the independent nature of each arts discipline.**

Professional development and the preparation of new teachers focus on two critical areas—teachers' knowledge and skills in specific arts disciplines and connections to be made between and among arts disciplines. Knowledge about and skills in the use of the basic elements of the arts disciplines deepen the teachers' and students' understanding of individual disciplines and provide points of contact and areas of contrast to the other arts and other core disciplines.

Through understanding an arts discipline in depth, one begins to make connections to the other arts. For example, although the idea varies by culture, one way in which mood can be established in the visual arts is through the use of color—the shadings, intensity, and relationships of a color to other colors. When this use is understood through experiences with color in painting, collage, or sculpture and through discussions on subtleties of meaning in uses of color, connections are made to the use of coloristic devices in other arts disciplines. In music, for example, single notes are prolonged, shortened, distorted, or intensified (much like shading) to evoke a particular mood; notes are arranged together, in harmony or in discord, to provide a sense of expectation or gloom; and rhythmic patterns are designed to provide a laconic background for a more exuberant melody.

3. *Process and product.* **Teachers of the arts focus on arts processes as well as on the arts product or performance.**

Learning lies in doing as well as in reflecting on what was done. Exploring the learning involved in obtaining the product or performance—through purposeful, reflective activities during the process of learning and in bringing the product or performance to fruition—is important.

The research of cognitive psychologists confirms that people learn by doing and that the process of doing often involves experimentation. The experimenter explores various methods to bring about a desired result. Through the process of experimentation, or exploration, students gain understanding of the depth of the knowledge and skills required by each of the arts disciplines. Through teacher-guided reflection on the product or performance, students understand the nature of the learning they have experienced.

Public recognition can be given to the process during public exhibitions or performances. Examples of beginning work and works in progress (through displays of drawings, photos, audiocassettes, or videotapes), along with the culminating works, give value to hard work, progress, and the process.

4. *Affective and cognitive aspects of the arts.* **Teachers of the arts understand and develop both the affective and cognitive aspects of the arts.**

Arts education requires the use of all the cognitive processes common to other academic disciplines. To those processes the arts add feeling. Although the ability to express emotion through the arts is regarded as the essence of the arts, the power of the arts to train the mind should not be undervalued.

When students learn by doing and exploring, they experience the joy, exhilaration, and thrill of creative accomplishment or full engagement as an audience member. They may develop goose bumps when emotions, connections, and insights are suddenly discovered in a performance or a work of art. These experiences expand students' knowledge and create in students a lifelong love and appreciation for the arts.

5. *World arts and cultures.* **Teachers of the arts include arts and cultures from many parts of the world in teaching and learning.**

It is important for all students, from their earliest school years, to know and respect the arts of all cultures. Preservice education and professional development that include knowledge of the arts of different racial, religious, and cultural groups are essential for those who teach dance, theatre, music, or the visual arts and for those who teach the arts indirectly through other academic subjects. A broad base of knowledge in the arts includes knowledge of varied world cultures; religious and ceremonial arts; and the American arts, such as musical theatre, mural painting, and jazz. Through these rich experiences teachers can see the arts from many different personal or cultural lenses, and the curriculum can reflect the multiplicity of sources from which American culture has derived its tremendous vigor.

6. *Cooperation.* **Teachers of the arts work cooperatively with colleagues, members of the arts community, and others responsible for arts education and provide opportunities for students to work and learn cooperatively.**

Arts programs at any grade level are successful when there is evidence of cooperation. Cooperation begins with the planning process, which involves the classroom teacher; arts specialists in dance, music, theatre, and the visual arts; and community artists, who later may be used in classroom instruction. These educators also articulate the program together with the other persons responsible for developing and confirming curriculum and resources: school and district administrators; curriculum specialists at the district and, perhaps, county levels; higher education faculty; community arts resource persons; teachers at other grade levels or departments; and librarians, who can help identify literature and technology resources. The same kind of cooperation and articulation follows through to the implementation of the program.

Goals for a comprehensive arts program include the development and implementation of a well-planned curriculum that meets the guidelines contained in this framework in each arts discipline; the integration and connection in a meaningful way of the arts curriculum throughout the arts program; and the establishment of the arts program in a prominent role in the core curriculum for all students. Programs improve through cooperation and articulation, and professional development takes place as the participants gain knowledge and skills from each other.

The collaborative nature of the planning process and teaching model provides an important example of collaborative learning for students.

7. *Assessment.* **Teachers of the arts design and score arts assessments, using a variety of methods.**

Student learning in each of the arts is assessable. Professional development that includes research in performance assessment— understanding the purpose of assessment, appropriate types of assessment, and the application of assessments to each of the arts—and the opportunity to develop and implement assessment strategies embedded in student learning strengthens curriculum and instruction. Assessment as a part of the instruction rather than an interruption in learning is instructionally sound. The design and scoring of assessments require practice. The process includes grounding lessons in framework-related content and developing and using scoring rubrics that reflect students' knowledge and skills in the four components of each arts discipline.

Teachers who are skilled in performance assessment at the classroom level also cooperate with others at the school and district levels to design assessments for accountability purposes.

8. *Technology.* **Teachers of the arts are knowledgeable about and use current electronic technologies.**

A teacher's ability to reach all students is maximized when that teacher keeps up on current research on the uses of technology in the arts and on technological resources in dance, theatre, music, and the visual arts; knows how to use new technologies as they emerge; and knows when best to use the resources. When teachers have frequent opportunities to learn about and use a variety of technologies, they become comfortable with the media, are willing to experiment, and can select the appropriate resources to meet various learning styles.

Appendixes

Appendix A

A Vision for the Arts in California Schools: Doing Right by Our Children

Elliot W. Eisner

THERE are few educational policy decisions that are more important in shaping the course of students' cognitive growth than defining what should be taught in our schools. Decisions made about the subjects that schools should teach not only define the content that students are to come to know; they shape the ideas and skills through which they structure their perception and comprehension of the world. Each subject, in its own special way, strengthens particular intellectual processes and provides the tools with which students come to experience and understand that world. For example, mathematics develops forms of reasoning that pertain to special structures and to the use of numerals for representing relationships within those structures. Reasoning in the visual arts and in music requires students to pay close attention to the ways in which image and sound are patterned. History and the social sciences develop forms of cognition that invite students to see connections between the arts, the sciences, and the values and forms of life that people lead. Thus, decisions taken about what should be taught in California schools are, in a very real sense, decisions about the kinds of minds that children will have the opportunity to create.

The idea that minds are created through the process of education is not one that is common. We tend to think about minds as biologically given entities that humans possess at birth. What *is* possessed at birth is brains: the physical capacity to interact with the environment for purposes of survival. It is with the aid of culture that children develop different kinds of mental skills and acquire attitudes towards the world. It is the curriculum and the quality of teaching that students receive that represent to the students the ways in which the world can be perceived and understood. In a sense, the curriculum is a mind-developing device, and educational

Elliot W. Eisner is Professor of Education and Art, School of Education, Stanford University.

policies pertaining to its aims and content express the values that are intended, one way or another, to guide the direction of its growth.

Given this conception of the relationship between educational policy, school curricula, and the development of cognition, questions about the content of school programs take on an extraordinary significance. This significance looms even larger when one considers that the choices that must inevitably be made are not infinite; time is limited and time in school runs out. Hence, given the importance of the decisions and the limits of time, policy makers have a crucial role to play in defining what matters.

I intend in this essay to provide a basis for thinking about those choices and, more specifically, for illuminating the special contributions that the arts can make to both the process we call education and to its ultimate consequences, the ways in which students learn to have and make sense of their experience.

To make this case, I must address fundamental questions about the relationship between the human sensory system and the student's conceptual ability. Conceptualization, in turn, needs to be related to the process of representation or symbol formation. I address these matters not to appear erudite or arcane but because I believe that without a solid theoretical foundation, the educational justification for any content area in the curriculum is unstable. Let us therefore begin.

Humans possess a sensory system that operates at birth and makes it possible for infants to experience aspects of the qualitative environment they inhabit. For the child, the world encountered is unnamed. It is essentially an array of qualities—sound,

sight, taste, touch. These qualities, as experienced within the limits of the infant's capacities, define the infant's world. Over time, through development, learning, and acculturation, the sensory capacities are refined or, in psychological terms, differentiated. As this occurs, the child becomes increasingly able to make finer and finer distinctions among the qualities of the world around him or her. Through this process the child learns to formulate images that represent in memory qualities of the world that were previously encountered. Eventually, for example, the child is able to recall the qualities that constitute the mother's face, the sound of the mother's voice, the particular touch the child experiences when held. As the child develops, the child acquires a memory that enables him or her to recall prior experience. It is by virtue of memory that general conceptions are formed. These general conceptions are simplified images held in the memory that stand for the particulars of individual experience. For example, we all have a general schema or image of things like houses, people, places, and so forth. Concepts are distillations of the multiple experiences we have had. Out of these experiences, we extract a set of common features that represent the basic structure of aspects of our experience and in doing so we engage in concept formation.

In the view I have just advanced, concepts are images whose forms appear in any of our sensory modalities. We have an auditory image of Baroque music, a visual image of a school, a gustatory image of grapes, and a tactile image of the feel and heft of a brick. We also have images of beauty, of courage, of kindness. These images are shaped by artists in the work they create. These images, in turn, influence our conceptual life. Concepts become meaningful not by virtue of possessing names, but by our being able to imagine the referents to which the names refer. When students cannot imagine or recall what a word refers to, learning is meaningless.

The images that populate our conceptual life not only can be recalled, but also can be treated imaginatively. That is, we are able to conceive of entities we have never directly encountered, entities that exist only in our mind's eye. We can think of unicorns and quarks, infinity and goblins. We are able to create images that allow us to consider or participate in possibilities that we ourselves create. While recall provides us with experience as it was, imagination provides us with access to experience as it might become. Hence, the development of the students' imaginative capacities is an extraordinarily important resource for sustaining the viability of a culture. It is imagination that makes growth in the sciences and in the arts possible. Without it, we would be left with only the ability to remember what was, but not to conceive of what might be.

The business of remembering, and even imagining, has no social significance unless in some way the content of our consciousness is transformed into some public form which makes it possible to share with others what it is that we have conceived. In every culture individuals have been afforded access to a variety of symbolic systems or forms of representation that enable them to give a public face to their private visions. Literal language, for example, is one of our most powerful and precise means for saying what is on our minds. But even language in its literal form, as powerful as it is, does not by any means exhaust the limits of language or satisfy our need to use other linguistic forms in order to do what the literal cannot. Poetry, for example, was invented to say, paradoxically, what words can never say. Poetic meaning transcends the literal. Similarly, literature was invented so that humans could use language to craft meanings that would convey to others what only the literary can convey. Literature and poetry, to consider only two examples, were made to meet those human needs that the literal use of language could not address.

Mathematics makes it possible to represent in the public world precise relationships having to do with space and quantity so that the practical needs could be met and the theoretical journeys that mathematical thought makes possible could be undertaken. Mathematics, like language, has both its instrumental utility and its intrinsic satisfactions: mathematics is both a tool and a toy.

The arts—the visual arts, music, theater, and dance—are and always have been powerful symbol systems that have made it possible for humans to make public meanings that they could not express. The visual arts, for example, enable children to represent what words cannot articulate. The visual arts are not only nonverbal, they are preverbal. They also afford children the opportunity to learn how to reason about the arrangement of visual qualities and, in the process, to learn how to see and assess the extent to which their work adequately portrays their intentions.

Unlike much of what is taught in schools, in the visual arts there is no single correct answer. Imagination matters. So does sensibility. So too does the ability to judge visual relationships and to improve them. The same, of course, can be said for music and the other arts. All of the arts depend upon the use of the human's most exquisite capacity—judgment. Looked at this way, the arts are not merely ornamental in education, they are fundamental resources through which the world is viewed, meaning is created, and mind is developed.

The kinds of cognitive processes that are invited and are developed through the process of crafting and perceiving images, whether visual, auditory, or kinesthetic, call upon the individual to learn to think within the medium he or she employs. The modes of intelligence that such curricular tasks foster can influence the kind of lives children are able to lead. Learning how to think about the qualities we call visual, auditory, and kinesthetic relates not only to the specific arts materials and tasks students encounter in school but also to the world of sight, sound, and movement found outside of schools. In fact, such qualities are considerably more ubiquitous than much of what is now taught in California schools. As virtuous as sentential calculus might be, the opportunities students have to think in the mode and content it employs are, for most, limited.

The world of vision, sound, and movement is a world within which we are steeped. It surrounds us, it envelops us, it is an ongoing part of our lives. The extent to which that world can be experienced is, however, significantly impacted by the skills that students have acquired. Their ability to experience what can be seen is not merely a function of "exposure." It is the result of skilled teaching, the existence of educational programs that acknowledge its importance and that provide the time necessary for children to learn how to see. Put more simply, these abilities must be developed by teachers using substantive curricula in schools.

The ideas I have presented so far are intended to help the reader grasp the meaning and implications of several major ideas. One of these is that policy decisions concerning what shall be taught in California schools are, at base, decisions about the kinds of opportunities children will have to invent their own minds. Second, the justification for the inclusion of any subject in the school curriculum ultimately rests upon a conception of how minds are developed and how meanings are made. Education is about the creation of mind and the expansion of meaning. Third, human experience depends initially upon the extent to which we have refined our sensory system. It is through the refined senses that we get in touch with the world. This, in turn, makes it possible to

form concepts. Fourth, once concepts are formed, they can be recalled or treated imaginatively. The imaginative treatment of our conceptual life makes it possible to create new possibilities that can be pursued. Fifth, the public realization of these possibilities requires the ability to skillfully use the various symbol systems or forms of representation that the culture itself makes available. Students, in a sense, become multiliterate as they learn how to use a variety of symbolic forms as means for either recovering or creating new meanings.

Given this view, it should be clear that the arts, along with the sciences, mathematics, history, and literal language, are major cultural resources for recovering and constructing meanings. Further, the meanings constructed within each of these forms are unique; they cannot be translated in an exact fashion to other forms. The arts are among the primary educational options available for schools; they are among the most demanding and informing forms that schools can make available.

This then, in brief, is the core of the argument. In addition to this conception of the role of arts, the arts have other important lessons to teach. I recite them here. First, the arts teach the young that not everything worth knowing can be put into words. We know more than we can say. Second, not all problems have single solutions. The arts, unlike much of what is taught in school, invite multiple and idiosyncratic solutions. There is no one way to arrive at a "correct" answer in any of the arts, nor is there one answer to arrive at. Third, the arts provide compelling testimony that feeling is not necessarily an impediment to thought. Indeed, the arts exploit the student's capacity to feel as a source and means of insight. Artistic forms make vivid those forms of feelings that give people who know how to "read" them access to the lives of others. Literature does this, as do music and the visual arts. Fourth, the arts teach that the universal is sometimes most vividly displayed in the particular. Works of art make it possible for the young to grasp meanings residing within a particular rendering of a particular work whose content, nevertheless, extends well beyond the parameters of that work. Poets, playwrights, painters, composers tell us about the world in general through the particular works that they create. For example, in his play *Death of a Salesman,* Arthur Miller helps us understand through Willy Loman what it feels like to be an unemployed salesman in middle age. The character is at once a unique individual and at the same time everyman. Claude Monet helps us see light. Martha Graham helps us discover what movement can be.

Fifth, the arts help children grasp the idea that the world in which they live can be the subject of their undivided attention and that the skilled exploration of its qualities can be both a source of meaning and a source of delight. Genuine perception is no mere recognition that simply assigns a label to a set of qualities. Perception is the sensitive exploration of the nuances that constitute the world to which the senses have access. Schools can help children learn how to access the world.

When they are taken seriously as a part of the educational agenda for children in California's schools, the ideas I have developed in this brief statement are formidable. One of the educational implications of these ideas pertains to the ways in which various subjects might be related to each other in order to exploit their capacities to shed light on ideas that matter. History–social science, an obvious candidate, can be designed so that works of literature, music, dance, and the visual arts all contribute to the students' understanding of a period in history, a culture, a people. Science can be better understood by the use of visual resources that make vivid the linguistic abstractions that are so prevalent in science texts.

The achievement of such education goals will, of course, depend upon both the development of programs that make such learning possible and the presence of teachers whose conception of the subject recognizes and embraces the range of its possibilities. It will also require the availability of materials that help teachers move into such teaching gradually. Put another way, the publication of lofty vision statements eloquently expressed is no substitute for making available the time, the materials, and most of all, the ability to reconceptualize what a curriculum might look like. It is the task of the curriculum framework committee to provide the leads and structures that will enable local school districts, schools, and individual teachers to build programs that help the students achieve the values that the initiating vision articulated.

My hope is that the lofty aims I have described and the theoretical rationale I have provided are not seen simply as academic window dressing, but as an initial plan that makes the confident justification of the arts in California schools possible. I also hope that these ideas live their educational lives in the practices that teachers employ in their classrooms. It is where the rubber hits the road that education really matters. All else is prologue. But prologues can provide direction and can yield insight. I hope that this prologue succeeds on both counts.

Appendix B

Criteria for Evaluating Instructional Resources for Visual and Performing Arts

*T*HE criteria for evaluating instructional resources in dance, music, theatre, and the visual arts for students in kindergarten through grade twelve shall reflect the philosophy and curriculum and instruction guidelines expressed in this edition of the *Visual and Performing Arts Framework.* High-quality print and nonprint instructional resources that meet the criteria will support the implementation of the framework.

Although the evaluation criteria that follow were developed for kindergarten-through-grade-eight state-level adoptions, they may also be useful at the local level in the evaluation of resources for use in kindergarten through grade twelve. School districts should also use this material to develop criteria for examining the extent to which resources support the implementation of a complete arts program throughout a specified period of time, as is promoted in the framework. In addition, the relevant portions of the California *Education Code* and the requirements stipulated in the *Standards for Evaluation of Instructional Materials with Respect to Social Content*[1] should be noted.

The criteria are divided into the following categories:

- Arts Content
- The Work Students Do
- Program Organization and Structure
- Arts for All Students
- Support for the Teacher
- Assessment

Each category offers a different perspective of the way in which the whole program should be experienced by the students. In using these categories, reviewers should keep in mind the following general points:

- The categories are not distinct; they are connected. For example, students' experiences in a program cannot be judged accurately simply by looking at the category titled "The Work Students Do." Students' experiences will also be affected by the quality of the teaching, the kinds of units and tasks worked on, and the content of the program.

---

[1] *Standards for Evaluation of Instructional Materials with Respect to Social Content.* Sacramento: California Department of Education, 1986.

- All the elements of an instructional program are to be examined in each category for how well they work together to provide a quality program for students in a classroom. The criteria described here do not presuppose the presence or absence of a particular program element. The materials used in programs might extend from entirely print to entirely nonprint. For example, it is possible to design a complete program that does not have a single student textbook or multiple booklets at its center. Similarly, videotapes, computer software, and other technology might or might not be included in a program or might be a complete program.

- The subpoints in each category are not necessarily of equal weight and should not be judged individually. Instead, they should be used to help identify the qualities that contribute to a category.

- Those who use these criteria must evaluate carefully how effective the instructional resources will be in the classroom. The resources need to be descriptive enough to help conscientious teachers implement a program that is aligned with this framework but should not be so tightly structured that teachers have little flexibility.

Arts Content

Instructional resources support the essential ideas and content goals described in this framework. The resources offer a breadth of knowledge, the skills, and sufficient opportunities for students to understand a single arts discipline in depth; and the organization of the resources promotes the four components in arts education discussed throughout the framework. The content supports an arts curriculum that builds on students' prior knowledge and skills. Instructional resources reflect the richness that many cultures bring to the arts and respect for the American culture and the diversity within it. The resources provide experiences that help students become artistically literate, both in creating and in responding to art.

Resources may focus on one of the arts disciplines (dance, music, theatre, visual arts), with integrated connections to the other arts disciplines and other core subjects, as appropriate. Or, at the other end of the spectrum, the resources may address all four arts disciplines, with integrated connections to other core subjects, as appropriate.

Instructional resources address the ideas embedded in the four components in arts education: artistic perception, creative expression, historical and cultural context, and aesthetic valuing. These components are common to each of the arts, but they also contain characteristics unique to each arts discipline.

Artistic Perception

This component addresses the processing of sensory information through elements unique to the arts. It provides students with the basic knowledge and skills necessary to communicate in each art form.

The resources provide opportunities for students to expand their abilities to observe, comprehend, and respond to the arts and to recognize structures, functions, and skills unique to the arts. Materials include the essential vocabulary of the arts.

Chapters 3 through 6 in the framework provide specific information about this component for each of the four arts disciplines (dance, music, theatre, and the visual arts).

Creative Expression

This component addresses the production of artworks, either by creating them or by performing the works of others. Emphasis is placed on the process of creating, including understanding how art is made and developing problem-solving skills and creativity, and on the finished product (acknowledgment of the final work produced).

The resources provide opportunities for students to create and perform art (individually and in groups); utilize the principles, processes, and structures of the art form; and create and communicate meaning through the art form.

Chapters 3 through 6 in the framework provide specific information about this component for each of the four arts disciplines (dance, music, theatre, and the visual arts).

Historical and Cultural Context

This component addresses students' understanding of the arts in the time and place of their creation, the importance of artists and their works, the effect of the arts on society, and the relationship of the arts to various cultures and societies.

The resources provide opportunities for students to study the work of creative artists, the evolution of those works, and the effects of the works on society in the past and in the present; to study art from many parts of the world; and to study the relationship of the arts to human history and culture.

Chapters 3 through 6 in the framework provide specific information about this component for each of the four arts disciplines (dance, music, theatre, and the visual arts).

Aesthetic Valuing

This component addresses the concepts of analyzing, making informed judgments, and pursuing meaning in the arts and students' understanding of the *power* of art and the human, emotional response to art.

The resources provide students with opportunities to analyze, interpret, and make critical judgments of works of art; use aesthetic principles to evaluate and improve works of art; and derive meaning and value from artistic experiences.

Chapters 3 through 6 in the framework provide specific information about this component for each of the four arts disciplines (dance, music, theatre, and the visual arts).

The Work Students Do

The resources provide students with work that is engaging and meaningful and focuses on the arts content as described in this framework. They provide students with opportunities to understand the intrinsic value of the arts and the value that the arts bring to cognitive and emotional growth. The resources provide the tools for exploration and communication and help students understand that the arts are and always have been a basic and central medium of human communication and understanding. The resources support the idea that through the arts students learn how to be creative, reasoning, thoughtful citizens.

The resources provide students with opportunities to develop subject-matter content knowledge and skills as the students confer meaning and explore societies' values and aspirations.

The instructional resources provide students with ongoing opportunities to construct meaning in many modes and forms. Resources generally begin with a big idea or question and contain instructional strategies to direct the students' understanding of the underlying concepts within the idea or question.

Skills are taught in the context of meaningful experiences that allow for creative expression. There are multiple opportunities for students to learn, practice, and build on prior knowledge and skills. The resources include opportunities to learn skills unique to each arts discipline, as highlighted in chapters 3 through 6 of the framework. Many tasks require time, deliberation, and reflection and continue for several days. On these extended assignments teachers find the resources helpful in setting clear criteria for student work, suggesting ways in which students can meet the criteria, and delineating learning expectations for students.

Instructional resources provide all students with opportunities for participation, recognition, and successful achievement. Students have opportunities to develop literacy, problem-solving, and decision-making skills; demonstrate creativity, flexibility, and communication skills; learn and use specialized language; and seek out the arts both for pleasure and as an avenue for human understanding.

Instructional materials in the arts include varied resources. Technology is represented throughout the curriculum in several ways. Students learn the impact of various forms of technology on the arts throughout time. In the creative process students use technology appropriate to their grade level and development and appropriate to the art form. Technology is incorporated into instructional activities. It provides access to the worldwide information network and multiple resources or collections and supports the creative and assessment processes.

Program Organization and Structure

Resources offer (1) an in-depth treatment of a single arts discipline, with meaningful connections to other arts disciplines and other core subjects; or (2) a substantive, integrated treatment of two or more of the arts disciplines. In each case opportunities for students to make connections to the other arts disciplines and to the other core subjects help extend the students' understanding of the subject.

Instructional resources demonstrate that the arts enrich and are enriched by other subjects. That means that the resources include connections to other arts disciplines and other core subjects, when appropriate to the knowledge and skills of the arts discipline under study.

The prose style of the instructional resources is lively and engaging. The language and vocabulary of the arts are age-appropriate and are introduced and used properly to enhance student understanding but are not allowed to dominate the purpose of learning.

The format and presentation of instructional resources are responsive to the needs and comprehension of students at the students' respective grade levels. For example, formatting materials with clear headings, subheadings, illustrations, photographs, graphs, and clearly labeled charts greatly increases the likelihood that students will understand basic concepts.

The content and length of audio materials (e.g., materials on records, compact discs, and tapes) and visual materials (e.g., slides, transparencies, art reproductions, photographs, videotapes, and materials on laser discs and CD-ROM) are appropriate for the age level of student learners and the instructional objectives for those learners. Sound quality is clear and possesses good fidelity, and visual materials provide clear images.

Technology-based resources can be integrally related to other instructional materials (i.e., as a necessary element of an instructional resources program); they can be used as supplementary resources; or they can be the sole resources for an instructional program. Electronic media meet the standards for exemplary technology and software as presented in the *Guidelines for Interactive Technology Resources in California Schools* and the *Guidelines for Instructional Video in California Schools*, both of which are available from the California Instructional Video Clearinghouse, Stanislaus County Office of Education, 801 County Center Three Court, Modesto, CA 95355-4490, telephone (209) 525-4993; and from the California Software Clearinghouse, California State University, Long Beach, 1250 Bellflower Boulevard, LA 1-201, Long Beach, CA 90840-1402, telephone (310) 985-1764.

Arts for All Students

Instructional resources provide opportunities for all students to become knowledgeable, discriminating, conscious, and demanding consumers and producers of the arts. Although all students may not choose the arts as a career, each student should have the opportunity to create, experience, and respond to the arts (dance, music, theatre, and the visual arts). Learning opportunities are enhanced by using nonverbal media (e.g., photos, illustrations, drawings, and demonstrations) to communicate. Instructional resources address the four components in arts education, which bring balance to the curriculum for each arts discipline and allow all students access to the arts curriculum.

Students gifted with creative aptitudes have the instructional resources to further develop their knowledge and skills.

Careers in the arts and the role of the arts in the economic development of California and the nation are explored.

The resources reflect strategies that have proved successful in engaging all students in active learning. The resources allow students to participate fully in each unit, and the varied thinking and meaning-centered tasks provide access for all students.

Instructional resources provide a common experiential base for all students, including students with special needs. Activities or additional resources that are provided for students having difficulty in some areas are in addition to, not instead of, the regular program.

Students with limited proficiency in English are not excluded from the study of the arts. Instructional resources present a perspective that respects the dignity and worth of all people, regardless of their differences, and build on the knowledge and cultural and linguistic foundations that students bring to class. Teachers' editions and reference resources provide ways in which teachers can make instruction for LEP[2] students compre-

hensible and appropriate, according to age and academic background. Providing materials in the primary languages of LEP students is one way of giving them access to the curriculum. Other ways include providing glossaries; summaries of important concepts; and directions, instructions, or problems and tasks in the students' primary languages.[3]

Support for the Teacher

Instructional resources describe the arts program so that teachers can implement it. The resources provide many suggestions specific to lessons and units as well as illustrative examples of ways in which the teacher can facilitate the student behaviors and learnings identified in the framework for each arts discipline. Suggestions for teachers are based on current research on learning styles and effective instruction.

The resources consistently focus on the essential ideas in this framework. They also contain suggestions for when information is to be presented to students; descriptions and visuals of what the instructional units look like in the classroom; and descriptions of the ways in which the experiences within units are related to what is known about students' learning or developmental levels.

Resources provide information on important things to do and say in a lesson or unit, including suggestions for questions to ask students and responses to encourage student engagement in the arts.

Resources provide teachers with models for assessing students in the arts, including performance assessments, and suggestions for using assessment results to tailor the instruction to students' needs.

---

[2] Although some publications and individuals refer to students who are learning English as *English-language learners* or *English learners,* this criterion uses the term *limited-English proficient* (LEP) because it is the one used in law. As the term is used here, LEP (limited-English and non-English-speaking) students are those who do not have the clearly developed English language skills of comprehension, speaking, reading, and writing necessary to succeed in the school's regular instructional programs.

[3] In 1994 the five largest language groups among LEP students in California, the groups that should be accommodated with resources, are (in rank order) Spanish, Vietnamese, Hmong, Cantonese, and Cambodian.

The resources provide suggestions for creating a positive classroom and school environment that supports a comprehensive arts program and acknowledge and support the parents' and the community's role in this environment.

Resources provide information for both teachers and students about how to use materials and equipment safely.

Resources give suggestions for working with a diverse classroom of students. These suggestions include alternative methods and techniques for tailoring the curriculum to the background and needs of the students while maintaining the integrity of the curriculum; examples of how best to adapt the presentation of information and skills to build on the strengths of the students and help students work together cooperatively; and methods for managing resources, including those that are based on technology, to ensure that they support meaningful student work and that students have access to the resources when the students need to use them.

Support for the teacher includes suggestions for ways in which to bring the students' world and daily experiences into the classroom so that students connect effectively with classroom arts activities. The resources support connections between and among the arts, between the arts and other curricular areas, and between the school and arts resources in the community. Examples of effective connections are provided. For example, partnerships between the school community and the professional artist, the educator-artist, community groups, institutes of higher learning, business and industry, and local arts agencies are encouraged; strategies for developing partnerships and examples of successful partnerships are provided.

Assessment

Assessment is consistently aligned with the instructional program described in this framework. Instructional resources at every grade must include frequent opportunities for performance assessments, which are usually embedded in the curriculum and instruction and pertain to each of the four components. The variety of assessment tasks include reflections and writing, projects, individual or group performance tasks or exhibitions, open-ended problems, and portfolios. Assessments are not limited to end-of-unit, end-of-course, or culminating performances or products. Assessment of work in progress enables student, teacher, and parents to appreciate the growth of the student's skills and the learning process. Assessments inform and assist the teaching-learning process. During assessments student should have the opportunity to use technology-based resources and other resources and references, as appropriate. Assessments should be designed to provide students with ample time in which to work on assessment tasks and opportunities to revise and resubmit projects to bring performance up to high-quality standards.

Specific suggestions for assessment should be included in units of work, although assessment activities may or may not be distinguished from learning tasks because of their similar characteristics. The resources should include general and frequent unit-specific suggestions to the teacher about models for assessing student performance and using assessment results to improve student performance and instructional practices. Other suggestions include using learning tasks for assessment purposes; observing, listening to, and questioning students while they work and tracking insights about students; organizing and using student portfolios; and involving students in self-assessment.

Parents should be kept involved in the educational progress of their children and informed about the variety of assessment methods being used.

Appendix C

Examples of Careers in the Visual and Performing Arts

This chart includes examples of careers in the arts or places in which artists might be employed. This is not an exhaustive list; it contains only a sample of the possibilities.

DANCE	MUSIC	THEATRE	VISUAL ARTS
Pre K–postsecondary educator/consultant:	*Pre K–postsecondary educator/consultant:*	*Pre K–postsecondary educator/consultant:*	*Pre K–postsecondary educator/consultant:*
Public/private schools	Public/private schools	Public/private schools	Public/private schools
Private studios	Private studios	Private studios	Private studios
Dance movement for—	Music for—	Community "little theatre"	Museums
Athletes (e.g., gymnasts, skaters)	Athletic events		School publications
Cheerleaders	Churches/synagogues		Universities and colleges
Physical education	Songleaders		
			Visual arts assessment
Dance assessment	Music assessment	Theatre assessment	Visual arts technology
Dance technology	Music technology	Theatre technology	
			Arts administrator:
Arts administrator:	*Arts administrator:*	*Arts administrator:*	Visual arts department in schools
Dance department in schools	Music department in schools	Theatre department in schools	Community arts councils
Community arts councils	Community arts councils	Community arts councils	Colleges and universities
Colleges and universities	Colleges and universities	Colleges and universities	Museums
Private studios	Performing ensembles	Private studios	Private studios
Professional groups and associations	Private studios	Professional groups and associations	Professional groups and associations
	Professional groups and associations		

Examples of Careers in the Visual and Performing Arts *(Continued)*

This chart includes examples of careers in the arts or places in which artists might be employed. This is not an exhaustive list; it contains only a sample of the possibilities.

DANCE	MUSIC	THEATRE	VISUAL ARTS
Dancer:	*Instrumentalist:*	*Actor/actress:*	*Visual artist:*
Amusement/theme park	Amusement/theme park	Amusement/theme park	Amusement /theme park designer
Ballet	Ballet or musical theatre	Dinner comedy	Animator
Ensemble	Band—	Film/television/video	Architect
Film/television/video	Armed forces	Night club	Billboard artist
Folk/ethnic	Community	Radio	Calligrapher
Jazz	Concert	Theatre—	Cartoonist
Modern/contemporary	Jazz	Dinner	Commercial/computer graphics artist
Night club	Rock	Musical	Engraver
Stage	Stage	Professional	Fashion designer
	Dance/nightclub	Resident	Film/television designer
Choreographer	Film/television/video/ radio	Stock	Glassblower
	Orchestra—	Touring	Greeting card artist
	Chamber music		Holographer
	Choir	*Playwright*	Illustrator
	Ensemble		Industrial designer
	Show		Jeweler
	Stage		Lithographer
	Theatre		Painter
			Photographer
	Vocalist:		Photojournalist
	Band		Picture framer
	Choir		Potter
	Choral group		Sculptor
	Chorus		Sign painter
	Concert		Silkscreen artist
	Ensemble		Site-specific arts designer
	Jingle singer		Stained glass artist
	Musical theatre		Textile/fiber designer
	Opera		Typographer
	Radio or television backup singer		Weaver
			Woodworker

Examples of Careers in the Visual and Performing Arts *(Continued)*

This chart includes examples of careers in the arts or places in which artists might be employed. This is not an exhaustive list; it contains only a sample of the possibilities.

DANCE	MUSIC	THEATRE	VISUAL ARTS
Director: Dance company Theatre	*Director/conductor:* Band Choir Choral Musical theatre Opera Symphony	*Director/producer:* Art event/presentation Casting Community little theatre Theatre company Theatrical production	*Director/producer:* Ad agency Art exhibition Gallery/museum Graphic design agency
Owner: Dance company Theatre	*Owner:* Amphitheatre Theatre	*Owner:* Theatre Theatre/film company Theatre supply business	*Owner:* Ad agency Exhibition space Gallery
Technical production: Business manager Costume designer Lighting designer Manager Public relations representative Sets/prop designer Special effects designer Stage manager Video technology expert Wardrobe dresser	*Technical production:* Business manager Costume designer Lighting/sound designer Manager Public relations representative Recording studio engineer Sets/prop designer Special effects designer Stage manager Video technology expert Wardrobe dresser *Songwriting/arranging:* Arranger Composer Copyist Film orchestrator Music editor Music director for television, video, radio Recording studio	*Technical production:* Business manager Costume designer Lighting/sound designer Manager Public relations representative Sets/prop designer Special effects designer Stage manager Video technology expert Wardrobe dresser	*Technical production:* Business manager Editor Exhibition director Installation designer Lighting designer Manager Public relations representative Scenic artist Sets/prop designer Special effects designer Video technology expert Wardrobe designer

Examples of Careers in the Visual and Performing Arts *(Continued)*

This chart includes examples of careers in the arts or places in which artists might be employed. This is not an exhaustive list; it contains only a sample of the possibilities.

DANCE	MUSIC	THEATRE	VISUAL ARTS
Business/management:	*Business/management:*	*Business/management:*	*Business/management:*
Advertising agency	Advertising agency	Advertising agency	Advertising agency
Costume store	Amphitheatre	Costume construction/ rental	Art supply store
Marketing/promotion	Marketing/promotion	Costume store	Convention/fair
Personal agency	Music store	Marketing/promotion	Gallery
Press agency	Musical theatre	Personal agency	Marketing/promotion
	Personal agency	Press agency	Museum
	Press agency	Prop construction/rental	Press agency
		Scenic construction/ rental	
		Sets store	
Notator:	*Notator:*		
Autographer	Autographer		
Notator	Notator		
Reconstructor	Reconstructor		
Criticism/research:	*Criticism/research:*	*Criticism/research:*	*Criticism/research:*
Consumer researcher	Consumer researcher	Consumer researcher	Consumer researcher
Ethnologist	Ethnomusicologist	Ethnologist	Ethnologist
Historian/researcher	Historian/researcher	Historian/researcher	Historian/researcher
Librarian	Librarian	Librarian	Librarian
Textbook writer	Textbook writer	Textbook writer	Textbook writer
Writer/editor/critic for magazine or newspaper	Writer/editor/critic for magazine or newspaper	Writer/editor/critic for magazine or newspaper	Writer/editor/critic for magazine or newspaper
Medicine/science:	*Medicine/science:*	*Medicine/science:*	*Medicine/science:*
Dance medicine therapy	Therapist	Therapist	Illustrator— Medical texts Scientific texts
			Art therapist
Media:	*Media:*	*Media:*	*Media:*
Computer programmer	Computer programmer	Computer programmer	Computer programmer
Television consultant	Radio disc jockey	Television consultant	Television consultant
Video consultant	Television consultant	Video consultant	Video consultant
	Video consultant		

Examples of Careers in the Visual and Performing Arts *(Continued)*

This chart includes examples of careers in the arts or places in which artists might be employed. This is not an exhaustive list; it contains only a sample of the possibilities.

DANCE	MUSIC	THEATRE	VISUAL ARTS
Government services:	*Government services:*	*Government services:*	*Government services:*
Arts councils—	Arts councils—	Arts councils—	Arts councils—
National/state	National/state	National/state	National/state
Regional	Regional	Regional	Regional
Cultural arts commissions—	Cultural arts commissions—	Cultural arts commissions—	Cultural arts commissions—
National/state	National/state	National/state	National/state
Regional/local	Regional/local	Regional/local	Regional/local
Education consultant/ specialist	*Education consultant/ specialist*	*Education consultant/ specialist*	*Education consultant/ specialist*
Recreation:	*Recreation:*	*Recreation:*	*Recreation:*
Boys/girls clubs	Boys/girls clubs	Boys/girls clubs	Boys/girls clubs
Fitness/health clubs	Parks/recreation programs	Parks/recreation programs	Parks/recreation programs
Parks/recreation programs	Private camps	Private camps	Private camps
Private camps	YMCA/YWCA	YMCA/YWCA	YMCA/YWCA
YMCA/YWCA			
Designer:	*Designer:*	*Designer:*	*Designer:*
Costumes	Costumes	Costumes	Advertising
Lighting	Instruments	Lighting	Art materials/supplies
Sets/stage	Lighting	Makeup	Audiovisual
	Sets/stage	Model making	Automobile
	Sound	Props	Costumes/masks
		Sets/stage	Display
		Sound	Environmental
		Special effects	Exhibit
			Graphics
			Interior
			Jewelry
			Leather goods
			Package
			Pottery
			Sets/stage
			Textile
			Tools
			Toys
			Urban
			Wallpaper
			Window

Religion in the Public School Curriculum: Questions and Answers

  How should religious holidays be treated in the classroom?

Teachers must be alert to the distinction between teaching about religious holidays, which is permissible, and celebrating religious holidays, which is not. Recognition of and information about holidays may focus on how and when they are celebrated, their origins, histories, and generally agreed-upon meanings. If the approach is objective and sensitive, neither promoting nor inhibiting religion, this study can foster understanding and mutual respect for differences in belief.

Teachers will want to avoid asking students to explain their beliefs and customs. An offer to do so should be treated with courtesy and accepted or rejected depending on the educational relevancy.

Teachers may not use the study of religious holidays as an opportunity to proselytize or to inject personal religious beliefs into the discussion. Teachers should avoid this by teaching through attribution; for example, by reporting that "some Buddhists believe . . ."

From *Religion in the Public School Curriculum: Questions and Answers.* Isla Vista: California 3Rs Project: Rights, Responsibilities, and Respect (sponsored by the Curriculum and Instruction Steering Committee), n.d.

May religious symbols be used in public school classes?

The use of religious symbols, provided they are used only as examples of cultural or religious heritage, is permissible as a teaching aid or resource. Religious symbols may be displayed only on a temporary basis as a part of the academic program. Students may choose to create artwork with religious symbols, but teachers should not assign or suggest such creations.

  May religious music be used in public schools?

Sacred music may be sung or played as a part of the academic study of music. School concerts that present a variety of selections may include religious music. Concerts should avoid programs dominated by religious music, especially when these coincide with a particular religious holiday.

The use of art, drama, or literature with religious themes also is permissible if it serves a sound educational goal in the curriculum, but not if used as a vehicle for promoting religious belief.

  What about Christmas?

Decisions about what to do in December should begin with the understanding that public schools may not sponsor religious devotions or celebrations; study about religious holidays does not extend to religious worship or practice.

Does this mean that all seasonal activities must be banned from the schools? Probably not; and in any event, such an effort would be unrealistic. The resolution would seem to lie in devising holiday programs that serve an educational purpose for all students—programs that make no students feel excluded or identified with a religion not their own.

Holiday concerts in December may appropriately include music related to Christmas and Hanukkah, but religious music should not dominate. Any dramatic productions should emphasize the cultural aspects of the holidays. Nativity pageants or plays portraying the Hanukkah miracle are not appropriate in the public school setting.

In short, while [schools may recognize] the holiday season, none of the school activities in December should have the purpose, or effect, of promoting or inhibiting religion.

What about religious objections to some holidays?

 Students from certain religious traditions may ask to be excused from classroom discussions or activities related to particular holidays. Some holidays considered by many people to be secular (for example, Halloween and Valentine's Day) are viewed by others as having religious overtones.

Excusal requests may be especially common in the elementary grades, where holidays are often marked by parties and similar nonacademic activities. Such requests are routinely granted.

In addition, some parents and students may make requests for excusals from discussions of certain holidays even when treated from an academic perspective. If focused on a limited, specific discussion, such requests may be granted in order to strike a balance between the student's religious freedom and the school's interest in providing a well-rounded education.

Administrators and teachers should understand that a policy or practice of excusing students from a specific activity or discussion cannot be used as a rationale for school sponsorship of religious celebration or worship for the remaining students.

Appendix E

Facilities and Resources for a Comprehensive Arts Education Program

*F*EW schools now have budgets for a complete complex of facilities for teaching all four of the arts. But schools need to aspire to providing professional-quality experiences for students at every grade level. Students deserve to learn in the best conditions on and off campus. Schools should work toward providing the necessary facilities and equipment to bring about those conditions.

The elementary school classroom needs to provide the following resources:

- Arts textbooks and other media
- Storage for pictures, drawings, models
- Sinks for cleanup
- Instrument storage rooms
- Storage for robes, costumes, and props
- Stage and multipurpose room for performances
- Technology equipment, such as computers, scanners, monitors, software, printers

Middle schools and high schools need all the items noted above as well as the following:

- Acoustically satisfying rehearsal rooms for musical ensembles of all sizes, including solo performers

- Large rooms with resilient, sanded wooden floors; mirrors; and bars
- One stage (at least) with complete lighting, sound amplification, and mixing equipment
- Photographic studios and darkrooms
- Movie and television studios with editing equipment
- High-quality audio systems and sound-recording equipment
- Studios with easels, large tables, pottery wheels, kilns, and carving tools
- Galleries and display facilities
- Other new and pertinent electronic equipment, such as video toasters

The classroom itself is an important facility. Arts education can and needs to take place in the classroom, which is a complement to the specialized environments necessary for production and performance. Computers, videodisc players, videocassette recorders (VCRs), televisions, compact-disc players, and stereos need to be available in every classroom, with collections of software programs, videodiscs, and tapes for reference. Classrooms need to be decorated with examples of artistic products by students, guest artists, and artists in residence or with good reproductions.

Resources in school libraries should include comprehensive collections of books, media (CD-ROMs, audio- and videocassettes, computer diskettes), and reproductions.

Many arts resources are available electronically. Through the Internet, the worldwide electronic network, students and teachers can access information, such as archives, music recordings, libraries, and source documents, from around the world; compose music jointly by sending sound clips to one another; and communicate with artists and art historians directly to ask questions and collaborate on studies. Schools need viewing facilities and computers so that students have access to this wealth of information.

Renewable materials, such as paints, clay, makeup, or musical instruments, must be adequately budgeted to ensure that materials are available when students need them.

General Arts References

The Arts: A Competitive Advantage for California. Prepared by the Policy Economics Group. Sacramento: KMPG Peat Marwick and the California Arts Council, 1994.

The Arts and Cognition. Edited by David Perkins and Barbara Leondar. Baltimore: Johns Hopkins University Press, 1977.

Arts Education and NAEP: Developing a Consensus Framework for the NAEP Assessment of Arts Education in 1996. Washington, D.C.: National Assessment of Educational Progress, 1992.

Arts Education Assessment Framework. Washington, D.C.: The National Assessment Governing Board (NAGB), 1994. Describes the development of the 1996 NAEP *Arts Education Framework* and discusses the arts in United States education, the content and processes of the arts, desired attributes of the arts education assessment, and preliminary achievement-level descriptions.

Arts Education Research Agenda for the Future. Prepared by Pelavin Associates, Inc., for the National Endowment for the Arts. Washington, D.C.: U.S. Department of Education, 1994. Addresses some of the questions raised by arts educators, researchers, and the broader community on basic issues in arts education. Attempts to place arts education and assessment in the larger context of national education reform.

The Arts in America, 1992: A Report to the President and to the Congress. Washington, D.C.: National Endowment for the Arts, 1992

Barthe, Patte. "Selling Arts Literacy," *Basic Education*, Vol. 33 (March, 1989), 8–10.

Beyond Creating: The Place for Art in America's Schools. Santa Monica, Calif.: The J. Paul Getty Trust Publications, 1985. Contains seven case studies of selected school districts. Approaches art education as fundamental to a child's learning and supports the assumption that art is basic to education.

Caught in the Middle: Educational Reform for Young Adolescents in California Public Schools. Sacramento: California Department of Education, 1987. Contains recommendations for achieving educational reform and renewal within 22 principles of middle grades education. The recommendations are directed to those who occupy leadership roles and who have authority and power to give meaning and substance to the reform of middle grades education.

Down, A. Graham. "The Arts as the Vanguard of Reform," *Basic Education,* Vol. 33 (March, 1989), 6–7.

Eaton, Marcia M. *Basic Issues in Aesthetics.* Belmont, Calif.: Wadsworth Publishing Co., 1988. Discusses aesthetics clearly and makes complex issues accessible to novices. The material is organized around the components of an aesthetic situation and includes the roles of objects, makers, and audiences; the nature of interpretation, criticism, and aesthetic response; the languages and contexts of art; and the nature of aesthetic value.

Eisner, Elliot W. "The Arts as a Way of Knowing," *Principal,* Vol. 60, No. 1 (September, 1980), 11–14.

Eisner, Elliot W. *The Enlightened Eye: Qualitative Inquiry and the Enhancement of Educational Practices.* Old Tappan, N.J.: Macmillan Publishing Co., Inc., 1991.

Eisner, Elliot W. "The Invention of Mind: Technology and the Arts," *The Education Digest,* Vol. 49, No. 1 (September, 1983).

Eisner, Elliot W. *The Role of Discipline-Based Art Education in America's School.* Santa Monica, Calif.: The J. Paul Getty Trust Publications, 1988.
Investigates the arts and the mission of education and the status of art in the schools. It also describes discipline-based art education and discusses the function of the arts in schools and the role of evaluation.

Fowler, Charles. *Can We Rescue the Arts for America's Children? Coming to Our Senses 10 Years Later.* New York: American Council for the Arts, 1988.

Gardner, Howard. *Art, Mind and Brain: A Cognitive Approach to Creativity.* New York: Basic Books, 1984.

Gardner, Howard. *Creating Minds: An Anatomy of Creativity Seen Through the Lives of Freud, Einstein, Picasso, Stravinsky, Eliot, Graham, and Gandhi.* New York: Basic Books, 1993.

Gardner, Howard. *Frames of Mind: The Theory of Multiple Intelligences* (Tenth anniversary edition). New York: Basic Books, Inc., 1993.

Gardner, Howard. *Multiple Intelligences: The Theory in Practice.* New York: Basic Books, 1993.

Guide and Criteria for Program Quality Review—Elementary. Sacramento: California Department of Education, 1994.

Guide and Criteria for Program Quality Review—Middle Level. Sacramento: California Department of Education, 1994.

Handbook for Planning an Effective Visual and Performing Arts Program. Commissioned by the Curriculum and Instruction Steering Committee of the California Association of County Superintendents of Schools. Visalia, Calif.: Tulare County Office of Education, 1990.
Explains why planning is necessary and includes chapters on conducting a needs assessment and developing the organizational groups to establish goals and implementation strategies for K–12 arts education programs.

Holdren, John. "The Limits of Thematic Instruction," *Common Knowledge: A Newsletter of the Core Knowledge Foundation,* Vol. 7, No. 4 (Fall, 1994).

It's Elementary! Elementary Grades Task Force Report. Sacramento: California Department of Education, 1992.
Focuses on the changing school population, changing expectations for the elementary school, and the changing view of how children learn. The report points the way for elementary education reform to help bring a rich and rigorous education to all students.

Kaegan, Stephen S. *Aesthetic Persuasion: Pressing the Cause of Arts Education in American Schools.* Santa Monica, Calif.: The J. Paul Getty Trust Publications, 1990.

Kearns, Lola H.; Mary Taylor Ditson; and Bernice Gottschalk Roehner. *Readings: Developing Arts Programs for Handicapped Students.* Harrisburg: Arts in Special Education Project of Pennsylvania, Pennsylvania Department of Education, 1983.

Kent, Corita, and Jan Steward. *Learning by Heart: Teachings to Free the Creative Spirit.* New York: Bantam Books, 1992.

Kornblum, Rena Beth. *A Perceptuo-Cognitive-Motor Approach to the Special Child.* Harrisburg: Arts in Special Education Project of Pennsylvania, Pennsylvania Department of Education, 1982.

Lehman, Paul R. "What Students Should Learn in the Arts," in *Content of the Curriculum (1988 ASCD Yearbook)*. Alexandria, Va.: Association for Supervision and Curriculum Development, 1988, pp. 109–131.

Moore, Ronald. *Aesthetics for Young People*. Reston, Va.: National Art Education Association, 1995.

Moral, Civic, and Ethical Education and Teaching About Religion. Sacramento: California Department of Education, 1995.

Murray, Jon J. "Art, Creativity, and the Quality of Education," in *Fine Arts in the Curriculum*. Edited by Frederick B. Tuttle, Jr. Washington, D.C.: National Education Association, 1985, pp. 23–30.

National Standards for Visual and Performing Arts Education. Coordinated by Music Educators National Conference in collaboration with the American Alliance for Theatre and Education, the National Art Education Association, and the National Dance Association. Reston, Va.: Music Educators National Conference, 1994.
Establishes voluntary content and achievement standards for use by state, regional, and local arts organizations in the development of their own arts standards.

Norman, Donald A. *Things That Make Us Smart*. Reading, Mass.: Addison-Wesley Publishing Co., Inc., 1993.

Parsons, Michael J., and H. Gene Blocker. *Aesthetics and Education*. Champaign: University of Illinois Press, 1993.

Postman, Neil. *Technopoly: The Surrender of Culture to Technology*. New York: Random House, Inc., 1993.

The Power of the Arts to Transform Education: Summary Report. Washington, D.C.: Arts Education Partnership, John F. Kennedy Center for the Performing Arts, and the J. Paul Getty Trust, 1993.

Remer, Jane. *Changing Schools Through the Arts: How to Build on the Power of an Idea*. New York: American Council for the Arts, 1990.
Presents a convincing case for the role of the visual arts, music, dance, drama, architecture, and aesthetics in educating students. The discussion ranges from the value of the arts for their own sake to the usefulness of the arts in enhancing other fields and in kindling students' interest in learning.

Second to None: A Vision of the New California High School. Sacramento: California Department of Education, 1992.
Challenges schools to connect more students to higher-level learning experiences. The report calls for a strong academic foundation in the first two years of high school and demanding yet flexible program majors for students in grades eleven and twelve.

Shlain, Leonard. *Art and Physics: Experiments in Space, Time, and Light*. New York: William Morrow and Co., Inc., 1991.

Strengthening the Arts in California Schools: A Design for the Future. Sacramento: California Department of Education, 1990.
Presents ten recommendations of the Arts Education Task Force, describing specific actions necessary to develop comprehensive programs in the arts in schools throughout the state.

Toward a New Era in Arts Education. Edited by John McLaughlin. New York: American Council for the Arts, 1988.

Toward Civilization: A Report on Arts Education. Washington, D.C.: National Endowment for the Arts, 1988.
A wide-reaching and influential report. Describes how the arts are included in the classroom at all levels and discusses testing and evaluation in the arts, the preparation of teachers of the arts, and the

role of the National Endowment for the Arts in facilitating progress.

Wakefield, John F. "Creativity and Cognition: Some Implications for Arts Education," *Creativity Research Journal,* Vol. 2 (Spring, 1989), 51–83.

What Work Requires of Schools: A Scans Report for America 2000. Upland, Pa.: Diane Publishing Co., 1993.

Wolf, Dennie Palmer, and Joan Boykoff Baron. "Standards, Curriculum, and Assessment in Arts Education: Envisioning New Possibilities," in *Measuring Up to the Challenge.* Edited by Ruth Mitchell. New York: American Council for the Arts, 1994.
Report of the American Council for the Arts symposium held in Atlanta, Georgia, September 18–20, 1992.

World Class Standards for American Education. Prepared by the U.S. National Education Goals Panel. Washington, D.C.: U.S. Department of Education, 1992 (pamphlet).

Assessment in the Arts

Arts Propel: A Handbook for Music. Cambridge, Mass.: Educational Testing Service and Harvard Project Zero, 1992.
Discusses the evolution and establishment of the *Propel* process for teachers and administrators who are considering adopting *Propel* in their classrooms or school systems. The handbook centers on replicable music activities developed by teachers in the Pittsburgh (Pennsylvania) public school system. The publication titled *Arts Propel: A Handbook for Visual Arts* is also available.

Berlak, Harold. *Toward a New Science of Educational Testing and Assessment.* Albany: State University of New York Press, 1992.

Brandt, Ron. "On Assessment in the Arts: A Conversation with Howard Gardner," *Educational Leadership,* Vol. 45, No. 4 (December, 1987/January, 1988), 30–34.
Discusses the endeavors of Harvard's Project Zero, working in conjunction with the Educational Testing Service and the Pittsburgh schools, to develop meaningful assessment techniques for the arts.

The Challenge to Reform Arts Education: What Role Can Research Play? Edited by David Pankratz and Kevin V. Mulcahy. New York: American Council for the Arts, 1989.

Hurwitz, Al. "What Happens on Portfolio Day," *School Arts,* Vol. 89, No. 8 (April, 1990), 46–47.
Discusses the evaluation of high school arts students' portfolios by examiners from the admissions offices of art schools. Critiques range from general to specific impressions of the work. The article suggests that art teachers help their students be prepared to accept criticism.

In the Process: A Visual Arts Portfolio Assessment Pilot Project. Carmichael: California Art Education Association, 1991.
Documents assessment projects and examples of classroom practices of participating teachers throughout California.

Innovative Assessment: Portfolio Resources Bibliography. Portland, Ore.: Northwest Regional Educational Laboratory, 1993.
Contains annotated references to documents, journal articles, and books pertaining to all areas of assessment. Includes an index to help locate resources for assessment in the arts.

Measuring Up to the Challenge: What Standards and Assessment Can Do for Arts Education. Edited by Ruth Mitchell. New York: American Council for the Arts, 1994.

Contains papers presented at a symposium titled "Arts Education Assessment Action Agenda: Student Performance and Learning Outcomes," held by the American Council for the Arts in Atlanta, Georgia, in September, 1992. The report provides a detailed look at current knowledge as a basis for assessment policy, describes arts education assessment now being developed or implemented, and proposes policy directions.

Meeting the Challenge—The Schools Respond: Final Report. Sacramento: California Department of Education, 1990.

Mitchell, Ruth. *Testing for Learning: How New Approaches to Evaluation Can Improve American Schools.* New York: The Free Press, 1992.

Mitchell, Ruth, and Amy Stempel. "Six Case Studies of Performance Assessment," in *Testing in American Schools: Asking the Right Questions.* Upland, Pa.: Diane Publishing Co., 1992.

The "Six Case Studies of Performance Assessment" is also available as a separate document from the Office of Technology Assessment, Washington, D.C.

Prelude to Performance Assessment in the Arts, Kindergarten Through Grade Twelve. Sacramento: California Department of Education, 1993.

Uses the four components of instruction and the goals (reworked as content standards) defined in the *Visual and Performing Arts Framework* (1989) as guidelines in discussing examples of assessments in the arts and the issues underlying performance assessment. The document is a report of the Toward Arts Assessment Project (TAAP), cosponsored with the Sacramento County Office of Education.

Wolf, Dennie Palmer. "Opening Up Assessment," *Educational Leadership,* Vol. 45, No. 4 (December, 1987/January, 1988), 24–29.

Discusses the first one and one-half years of the *Arts Propel* project and its effects on the thinking and reflection of participating teachers and students. The article focuses on the need to address many questions and problems that arise in evaluating students' work in the arts.

Wolf, Dennie Palmer. "Portfolio Assessment: Sampling Student Work," *Educational Leadership,* Vol. 46, No. 7 (April, 1989), 35–39.

Reviews the first two years of the *Arts Propel* project in which students assess their work in the arts in much the same way that working artists, musicians, and writers judge their own work. Portfolio development is inherent in this evaluative process.

Wolf, Dennie Palmer, and Nancy Pistone. *Taking Full Measure: Rethinking Assessment Through the Arts.* New York: College Entrance Examination Board, 1991.

Describes assessment projects in each of the arts: dance, drama, music, and the visual arts. The authors examine the varied approaches that arts teachers use to enhance the thinking skills of their students.

Zerull, David S. "Evaluation in Arts Education: Building and Using an Effective Assessment Strategy," *Design for Arts in Education,* Vol. 92, No. 1 (September/October, 1990), 19–24.

Outlines Bennet Reimer's seven modes of interaction with the arts and seeks to establish a vocabulary of arts assessment. Cautions against standardized testing in the arts.

Dance

Alter, Judy. *Stretch and Strengthen.* Boston: Houghton Mifflin Co., 1992.

Explains how to teach correct traditional dance techniques and how to adapt the techniques to the needs of differing body types; emphasizes injury prevention.

Blom, Lynn, and Tarin Chaplin. *The Intimate Act of Choreography.* Pittsburgh: University of Pittsburgh Press, 1982.
A guide to teaching dance composition appropriate for junior and senior high school students.

Boorman, Joyce. *Creative Dance in the First Three Grades.* New York: David McKay Co., Inc., 1969.
A guide to integrating creative dance into the curriculum to meet the developmental needs of pupils in kindergarten through grade three.

Cayou, Dolores Kirton. *Modern Jazz Dance.* Palo Alto, Calif.: National Press Books, 1971.
A guide to teaching Afro-Haitian jazz technique.

Cheney, Gay. *Basic Concepts in Modern Dance* (Third edition). Pennington, N.J.: Princeton Book Co., Pubs., 1989.
A guide to teaching modern dance techniques.

Ellfeldt, Lois. *A Primer for Choreographers.* Prospect Heights, Ill.: Waveland Press, Inc., 1988.
A guide to helping students improvise and choreograph a dance.

Hawkins, Alma M. *Moving from Within: A New Method of Dance Making.* Pennington, N.J.: A Cappella Books, 1991.
A guide to teaching choreography using internal, personal, and emotional forms of expression.

Humphrey, Doris. *The Art of Making Dances.* Pennington, N.J.: Princeton Book Co., Pubs., 1991.

An indispensable, basic guide to choreography.

Joyce, Mary. *First Steps in Teaching Creative Dance to Children.* Mountain View, Calif.: Mayfield Publishing Co., 1994.
Contains lesson plans and instructions appropriate for teaching pupils in elementary school.

Russell, Joan. *Creative Dance in the Primary School.* New York: Frederick A. Praeger, Publishers, 1968.
Presents appropriate lesson plans for students at each grade level; integrates motor development with cognitive and social developmental needs.

Stinson, Susan W. *Dance for Young Children: Finding the Magic in Movement.* Reston, Va.: The American Alliance for Health, Physical Education, Recreation, and Dance, 1988.

Weikart, Phyllis. *Around the Circle.* Ypsilanti, Mich.: High/Scope Press, 1987.
An early childhood and primary-grade teacher resource for incorporating music and movement in instruction. Provides developmentally appropriate, easy-to-use lessons.

Weikart, Phyllis. *Teaching Movement and Dance*: *A Sequential Approach to Rhythmic Movement* (Third edition). Ypsilanti, Mich.: High/Scope Press, 1989.
The text provides a teaching background and extensive directions for folk dances related to music recorded on records, tapes, and compact discs.

Weikart, Phyllis. *Teaching Movement and Dance: Intermediate Folk Dance.* Ypsilanti, Mich.: High/Scope Press, 1984.
Provides dances and instructions that correlate with extensive recorded materials.

Music

Andrews, Edward. *The Gift to Be Simple.*
New York: Dover Publications, Inc., 1962.
Contains an extensive description of the
musical life of the Shakers. Includes many
songs and a few dance instructions.

Bring Multicultural Music to Children.
Reston, Va.: Music Educators National
Conference, 1992.
Work in multicultural music demonstrated
by four presenters. The presentations were
videotaped live at recent MENC conferences and symposiums. Some segments
include live tapes of work with children.

Choksy, Lois, and others. *Teaching Music in
Twentieth-Century America.* Englewood
Cliffs, N.J.: Prentice Hall, 1985.
Presents descriptions of four approaches
used in North American schools to teach
music: Dalcroze, Kodaly, Orff, and
Comprehensive Musicianship. Each
approach or method is described by a
noted authority, and classroom strategies
are presented.

Frazee, Jane, and Kent Kreuter. *Discovering
Orff. A Curriculum for Music Teachers.*
Valley Forge, Pa.: European American
Music Distributors Corp., 1987.
An invaluable handbook—a must for
elementary school music teachers. Describes important practices in participation
designed by Orff. Stresses the importance
of facilitating student contributions at all
levels of ability.

George, Luvenia A. *Teaching the Music of
Six Different Cultures* (Revised edition).
Danbury, Conn.: World Music Press, 1988.
Contains an introduction to and an analy-
sis of music, including African, African
American, American Indian, Jewish,
Hawaiian, and Puerto Rican music.
Includes activities for student involvement
and bibliographic and audiovisual refer-
ences.

*Guidelines for Performances of School Music
Groups.* Reston, Va.: Music Educators
National Conference, 1986.
Contains recommendations for setting
performance expectations and dealing
with limitations of school music groups in
elementary, middle/junior high, and high
schools.

*Handbook of Research on Music Teaching
and Learning.* Edited by Richard Colwell.
New York: Schirmer Books, 1992.
Provides an overview of all areas of music
research related to teaching and learning.
Organizes material by topic and age level,
from early childhood through adulthood
and professional development. Contains
55 comprehensive reviews of research by
leading experts.

Harrison, Lois N. *Getting Started in Music.*
Englewood Cliffs, N.J.: Prentice Hall,
1988.
Discusses the development of concepts
related to the elements of music and
provides basic activities for involving
children in music.

Harvard Dictionary of Music (Second
edition, enlarged and revised). Edited by
Willi Apel. Cambridge, Mass.: Belknap
Press of Harvard University Press, 1968.
An authentic source for learning musical
terms and vocabulary.

Jessup, Lynne. *World Music: A Sourcebook
for Teachers.* Danbury, Conn.: World
Music Press, 1988.

Jones, Bessie, and Bess L. Hawes. *Step It
Down: Games, Plays, Songs, and Stories
from the Afro-American Heritage.* Athens:
University of Georgia Press, 1991.
Contains games and plays, clapping plays,
dances, house games and plays, outdoor
games, songs, and stories. Both the
historical meaning and Mrs. Jones'
description of the elusive quality that
comes from "playing it" give the material

its emotional feel. The rich language and wonderful body of folk material are an important part of the African American heritage.

Kartomi, Margaret J. *On Concepts and Classifications of Musical Instruments.* Chicago: The University of Chicago Press, 1990.

An exhaustive study of the nature of classification and classification applied to literary transmission and oral transmission.

Katz, Susan A., and Judith A. Thomas. *Teaching Creatively by Working the Word: Language, Music, and Movement.* Englewood Cliffs, N.J.: Prentice Hall, 1992.

An excellent resource for specialists as well as generalists. Considers language a unifying element, the medium through which all subjects are taught, with multiple inherent possibilities for the creative use of language. Encourages the use of creative processes in all areas of the curriculum through the complements of music and movement.

Malm, William P. *Music Cultures of the Pacific, the Near East, and Asia* (Second edition). Englewood Cliffs, N.J.: Prentice Hall, 1977.

Marcuse, Sibyl. *Musical Instruments: A Comprehensive Dictionary.* New York: W.W. Norton & Co., 1975.

An authentic source on musical instruments of the world.

Multicultural Perspectives in Music Education. Edited by Patricia Campbell. Reston, Va.: Music Educators National Conference, 1989.

Provides a pragmatic approach to teaching world music traditions in upper elementary school through high school. Covers music of East Asia, Southeast Asia, India, South America, Africa, Middle East, and Europe as well as music of European

American, African American, and Native American cultures. Includes an extensive resource list.

Nash, Grace C. *Creative Approaches to Child Development with Music, Language, and Movement: Incorporating the Philosophies and Techniques of Orff, Kodaly, and Laban.* Van Nuys, Calif.: Alfred Publishing Co., 1974.

Nash, Grace C. *Do It My Way—The Child's Way of Learning, Levels K Through Six: A Handbook for Building Creative Teaching Experiences.* Sherman Oaks, Calif.: Alfred Publishing Co., 1977.

An excellent resource for specialists and generalists. Presents learning activities that incorporate the tools of muscular, sensory, creative, and emotional learning and use the entire brain, muscles, senses, and imagination. Applies a four-step learning process, bringing together language, movement, and music to motivate, reinforce, and strengthen student learning. Correlates rhythmic expression, movement, language arts, arithmetic, ecology, singing, and playing.

NASM Handbook, 1989–1990. Reston, Va.: National Association of Schools of Music, 1989.

Nettl, Bruno. *The Study of Ethnomusicology.* Champaign: University of Illinois Press, 1983.

Nettl, Bruno, and others. *Folk and Traditional Music of the Western Continents* (Third edition). Englewood Cliffs, N.J.: Prentice Hall, 1989.

Opportunity-to-Learn Standards for Music Instruction: Grades PreK–12. Reston, Va.: Music Educators National Conference, 1994.

Contains recommendations for music program administrators on curriculum, scheduling, staffing, materials, equipment, and facilities to meet national standards.

Sadie, Stanley. *The New Grove Dictionary of Music and Musicians* (Sixth edition). In 20 volumes. New York: Groves Dictionaries, Inc., 1980.

The most complete and authoritative encyclopedic source for learning about musical terms, concepts, vocabulary, and musicians.

The School Music Program: A New Vision. Reston, Va.: Music Educators National Conference, 1994.

Schwadron, Abraham A. *Aesthetics: Dimensions for Music Education.* Washington, D.C.: National Education Association, 1967.

Seeger, Charles. "Judgment in the Critique of Music," in *Essays for a Humanist.* Van Nuys, Calif.: Theodore Front Musical Literature, 1977, pp. 261–76.

Serafine, Mary L. *Music as Cognition.* New York: Columbia University Press, 1988.

Teaching Music with a Multicultural Approach. Introduction by William M. Anderson. Reston, Va.: Music Educators National Conference, 1991.

Contains background information; lessons; music notations; and resource lists for African Americans, American Indians, Asian Americans, and Hispanic Americans.

Tenzer, Michael. *Balinese Music.* Berkeley, Calif.: Periplus Editions, 1992.

Contains splendid pictures and descriptions of instruments, ensembles, and customs.

Warner, Brigitte. *Orff Schulwerk: Applications for the Classroom.* Englewood Cliffs, N.J.: Prentice Hall, 1990.

Serves as a user's guide to Carl Orff's philosophy; describes a step-by-step teaching program based on the three musical elements: rhythm, melody, and harmony. For music specialists.

What Works: Instructional Strategies for Music Education. Edited by Margaret Merrion and Clifford Madsen. Reston, Va.: Music Educators National Conference, 1989.

Synthesis of research findings. Provides practical applications for music teaching and learning.

Wheeler, Laurence, and others. *Orff and Kodaly Adapted for the Elementary School.* Dubuque, Iowa: William C. Brown Pubs., 1984.

Theatre

Barranger, Milly S. *Theatre: A Way of Seeing* (Fourth edition). Belmont, Calif.: International Thomson Publishing, 1995.

An excellent and unique textbook. Introduces theatre, its history, physical form, literature, and production styles. Fully illustrated.

Belt, Linda, and Rebecca Stockley. *Improvisation Through Theatresports*: *A Curriculum to Teach Basic Acting Skills and Improvisation* (Third revised edition). Puyallup, Wash.: Thespis Productions, 1996.

Benedetti, Robert L. *The Actor at Work* (Sixth edition). Englewood Cliffs, N.J.: Prentice Hall, 1994.

An excellent basic text, with good chapters on voice, body, textual analysis, characterization, and rehearsal discipline.

Bibliography of Multicultural Theatre Resources. Edited by David Kahn. Los Angeles: California Educational Theatre Association, 1993.

Contains more than 500 entries, most of which are annotated, including a short list of journals and selected video references. Provides a tool for a more culturally inclusive theatre program.

Brockett, Oscar G. *History of the Theatre* (Seventh edition). Needham Heights, Mass.: Allyn and Bacon, Inc., 1994.

Covers world theatre history in detail. Is considered the most authoritative history of theatre available.

Bruder, Melissa. *A Practical Handbook for the Actor*. New York: Random House, Inc., 1986.

A succinct and fundamental book dealing with an actor's concerns. Includes examples of scenes relating to the responsibilities discussed. Easy to read.

Cook, Wayne. *Centerstage: A Curriculum for the Performing Arts, K–3, 4–6*. Palo Alto, Calif.: Dale Seymour Publications, 1993.

Presents a theatre curriculum designed to help students become more aware of themselves and their world and develop critical-thinking and problem-solving skills in all curriculum areas. The material is divided into six levels; each level has 30 sequential lessons that lead students and teachers from exploratory activities to fully developed creative dramatics. The resource provides suggestions for the teacher on grouping and classroom management, activities for children with special needs, resources, and connections to other content areas.

Corson, Richard. *Stage Makeup* (Eighth edition). Englewood Cliffs, N.J.: Prentice Hall, 1986.

Contains 400 illustrations, 23 plates of period hairstyles, and color charts of step-by-step procedures in theatrical makeup.

Dean, Alexander, and Lawrence Carra. *Fundamentals of Play Directing* (Fifth edition). Orlando, Fla.: Harcourt Brace College Pubs., 1989.

Provides basic rules of play directing, with emphasis on stage positions and blocking.

Engelsman, Alan. *Theatre Arts I*. St. Louis: Alpen and Jeffries Pubs., 1983.

A complete course in beginning acting.

Giannetti, Louis. *Understanding Movies* (Seventh edition). Englewood Cliffs, N.J.: Prentice Hall, 1995.

Breaks film into basic elements for analysis, with an extensive chapter on synthesis. Elements are illustrated with movie stills, with extensive explanation, a Hitchcock storyboard, and an annotated bibliography.

Hagen, Uta, and Haskel Frankel. *Respect for Acting*. Old Tappan, N.J.: Macmillan Publishing Co., Inc., 1973.

King, Ermyn. *The Projected Play Called Puppetry: Life-giving as Life-giver, An Organic Process*. Harrisburg: Arts in Special Education Project of Pennsylvania, Pennsylvania Department of Education, 1989.

McCaslin, Nellie. *Creative Drama in the Classroom* (Sixth edition). White Plains, N.Y.: Longman Publishing Group, 1996.

Provides many examples for creative drama in the elementary classroom and discusses the methodologies of creative drama, theatre games, and educational drama.

Meserve, Walter J. *An Outline History of American Drama* (Second edition). New York: Feedback Theatrebooks and Prospero Press, 1994.

Covers the theatre from America's earliest days to the present. Defines topics clearly in paragraph headings, making the book easy to read and browse through.

Motter, Charlotte K. *Theatre in High School: Planning, Teaching, Directing*. Lanham, Md.: University Press of America, in association with American Theatre Association, 1984.

Contains courses of study for beginning and intermediate play production and stagecraft and chapters on play selection, play analysis and evaluation, plays by Shakespeare, directing, assembly programs, audience education, and so forth.

Parker, W. Oren, and Harvey K. Smith. *Scene Design and Stage Lighting*. Orlando, Fla.: Harcourt Brace College Pubs., 1990.

A comprehensive instructional text, covering all aspects of technical theatre.

Salisbury-Wills, Barbara. *Theatre Arts in the Elementary Classroom, Kindergarten Through Grade Three* (Second edition). New Orleans: Anchorage Press, 1995.

Provides background information on drama in the classroom and organizes lessons in specific grade-level chapters. Relates the study to the National Standards for Theatre Education.

Salisbury-Wills, Barbara. *Theatre Arts in the Elementary Classroom, Grades Four Through Six* (Second edition). New Orleans: Anchorage Press, 1995.

Provides background information on drama in the classroom and organizes lessons in specific grade-level chapters. Relates the study to the National Standards for Theatre Education.

Shurtleff, Michael. *Audition: Everything an Actor Needs to Know to Get the Part*. New York: Walker and Co., 1984.

Spolin, Viola. *Theatre Games for Rehearsal: A Director's Handbook*. Evanston, Ill.: Northwestern University Press, 1985.

Describes the practical applications of games and exercises.

Stanislavski, Constantin. *Instant Acting*. New York: Theatre Arts Books, 1936.

The original source of what has come to be known as "the method." Presents the method as a dialogue between the director and student actors in a series of acting classes.

Stern, Lawrence. *Stage Management* (Fifth edition). Needham Heights, Mass.: Allyn and Bacon, Inc., 1995.

A useful book on the duties and role of the stage manager. Includes examples.

Sweet, Harvey. *Handbook of Scenery, Properties, and Lighting, Vol. I: Scenery and Props* (Second edition). Needham Heights, Mass.: Allyn and Bacon, Inc., 1994.

An excellent primer of technical theatre, filled with illustrations. Covers equipment, supplies, and production from the primitive to the sophisticated. Presents all the basic needs of stagecraft.

Whelan, Jeremy. *Instant Acting: A Revolutionary Acting, Rehearsal, and Audition Method for Beginners to Professionals*. Cincinnati: Betterway Books, 1994.

Approaches acting from the teacher's viewpoint. Interesting and not heavily intellectual. Offers a methodology for achieving realistic performance.

Visual Arts

Addiss, Stephen, and Mary Erickson. *Art History and Education*. Champaign: University of Illinois Press, 1993.

Anderson, Richard L. *Calliope's Sister: A Comparative Study of Philosophies of Art*. Englewood Cliffs, N.J.: Prentice Hall, 1990.

A scholarly book on art in the Western cultures and in numerous non-Western cultures, including those of Eskimos and Australian aborigines and cultures in India and Japan. Appropriate for the visual arts classroom and for the study of such disciplines as anthropology, sociology, and history.

Barrett, Terry. *Criticizing Art: Understanding the Contemporary*. Mountain View, Calif.: Mayfield Publishing Co., 1994.

Provides a framework for critically considering contemporary art through describing, interpreting, evaluating, and theorizing about art. Applies the principles of art criticism to art forms as a means of illustrating the author's ideas and theories of criticism.

Battin, Margaret P., and others. *Puzzles About Art: An Aesthetics Casebook.* New York: St. Martin's Press, 1989.

Uses specific cases to stimulate questions about art and aesthetics. Develops insight into aesthetic issues and allows students to test and challenge aesthetic theories.

Berger, John. *Ways of Seeing.* New York: Viking Penguin, 1977.

A collection of verbal and pictorial essays that questions the way in which people view their surroundings and suggests that their viewing may be altered by what they hear, know, and believe.

Brown, Maurice, and Diana Korzenik. *Art Making and Education.* Champaign: University of Illinois Press, 1993.

Csikszentmihalyi, Mihaly, and Rick E. Robinson. *The Art of Seeing: An Interpretation of the Aesthetic Encounter.* Santa Monica, Calif.: The J. Paul Getty Trust Publications, 1990.

An intense yet readable examination of the aesthetic experience from a variety of points of view, including the major dimensions, a quantitative analysis, the form and quality, and methods for facilitation of the experience.

Discipline-Based Art Education: Origins, Meaning, and Development. Edited by Ralph A. Smith. Champaign: University of Illinois Press, 1989.

Hevey, David. *The Creatures That Time Forgot: Photography and Disability Imagery.* New York: Routledge, Chapman and Hall, Inc., 1992.

Hurwitz, Al, and Michael Day. *Children and Their Art: Methods for the Elementary School* (Fifth edition). Orlando, Fla.: Harcourt Brace College Pubs., 1991.

Lewis, Samella. *Art: African American* (Second revised edition). Los Angeles: Hancraft Studios, 1990.

A survey of African American art history from slavery to contemporary times.

Lippard, Lucy. *Mixed Blessings: New Art in Multicultural America.* New York: Pantheon Books, 1990.

Uses a survey and a philosophical approach to a look at the new art from a multicultural perspective.

Lonker, Sherrie. *A Sensorial Approach to Art: Pre-Art Discovery with Severely and Profoundly Impaired Children.* Harrisburg: Arts in Special Education Project of Pennsylvania, Pennsylvania Department of Education, 1982.

Mittler, Gene. *Art in Focus.* Westerville, Ohio: Glencoe, 1994.

Mount, Marshall W. *African Art: The Years Since 1920.* New York: Da Capo Pr., Inc., 1989.

Describes contemporary African artists and the arts of Africa.

Parsons, Michael J., and H. Gene Blocker. *Aesthetics and Education.* Champaign: University of Illinois Press, 1993.

Perkins, David N. *The Intelligent Eye: Learning to Think by Looking at Art.* Santa Monica, Calif.: The J. Paul Getty Trust Publications, 1994.

Read, Herbert. *Education Through Art.* New York: Pantheon Books, 1956.

Roukes, Nicholas. *Art Synectics.* Worcester, Mass.: Davis Publications, Inc., 1982.

Describes a form of creative thinking that combines imagination and analogical

thinking to transform familiar, common-place elements into new and exciting structures.

Rubinstein, Charlotte S. *American Women Artists: From Early Indian Times to the Present.* New York: Avon Books, 1982.

A historical survey of American women artists from early Native American times to the present.

Schuman, Jo Miles. *Art from Many Hands.* Worcester, Mass.: Davis Publications, Inc., 1984.

Provides background information on traditional art forms around the world, with directions for re-creating the art forms in the classroom.

Wachowiak, Frank, and Robert D. Clements. *Emphasis Art: A Qualitative Art Program for Elementary and Middle Schools* (Fifth edition). New York: HarperCollins College, 1993.

Useful for generalists as well as specialists. Four chapters are of particular interest: "Teaching Strategies"; "Evaluation of Children's Art"; "Avenues to Art Appreciation"; and "Art for Children with Special Needs."

Professional Development Resources

American Alliance for Theatre and Education, Arizona State University, Theatre Department, P.O. Box 872002, Tempe, AZ 85287-2002, (602) 965-6064.

California Arts Council, 1300 I St., Suite 930, Sacramento, CA 95814, (916) 322-6555.

The California Arts Project, P. O. Box 4925, San Rafael, CA 94913, (415) 499-5893.

Educational Theatre Association, 3368 Central Parkway, Cincinnati, OH 45225, (513) 559-1996.

The Getty Center for Education in the Arts, 401 Wilshire Boulevard, Suite 950, Santa Monica, CA 90401-1455, (310) 395-6657.

The John F. Kennedy Center for the Performing Arts, Washington, DC 20566-0001, (800) 444-1324.

Music Educators National Conference, 1806 Robert Fulton Drive, Reston VA 22091, (703) 860-4000.

National Art Education Association, 1916 Association Drive, Reston, VA 22091, (703) 860-8000.

National Dance Association, 1900 Association Drive, Reston, VA 22091-1502, (703) 476-3436.

National Endowment for the Arts, Nancy Hanks Center, 1100 Pennsylvania Avenue, NW, Washington, DC 20506-0001, (202) 682-5400.

National Endowment for the Humanities, 1100 Pennsylvania Avenue, NW, Washington, DC 20506, (202) 606-8400.

The following professional arts education associations change officers periodically. For the current telephone numbers and names of contact persons, call the California Department of Education, Curriculum Frameworks and Instructional Resources Office, at (916) 657-3023.

California Alliance for Arts Education

California Art Education Association

California Dance Education Association

California Education Theatre Association

California Humanities Association

California Music Educators Association